Front of House

Observations from a Decade on the Aisle

Denise Reich

phasmatis lux

Front of House : Observations from a Decade on the Aisle.
Copyright © 2015 by Denise Elizabeth Reich.

All rights reserved. No part of this book may be copied, transmitted, posted or reproduced in any manner whatsoever without written permission from the author except in the case of brief quotations embodied in critical articles or reviews.

Phasmatis Lux
phasmatislux@gmail.com
Walnut, CA, USA

Electronic book available from Bear Manor Media
www.bearmanormedia.com

Cover design © Denise E. Reich.
Interior formatting by Denise E. Reich from book template
by Derek Murphy, www.creativeindie.com.

Easter Bonnets performance photograph © 2006 Broadway Cares/Equity Fights AIDS. All rights reserved. Used with permission of BC/EFA.

David Belasco portrait from public domain source : *The Life of David Belasco* by William White, 1918.

All additional photos © Denise E. Reich. All rights reserved.

Note on the text : This book uses « theater » to refer to the building itself or to the art form, and « theatre » to refer to the proper name of a venue. A few venues mentioned in the text have names which deviate from this convention; the book uses their spelling.

Names of non-celebrity individuals have been changed for privacy.

Publisher's Cataloging-in-Publication Data
Reich, Denise E.
Front of house: observations from a decade on the aisle/Reich, Denise E.
Includes bibliographical references.
ISBN-10   0692483020
ISBN-13   978-0692483022
1. Reich, Denise E. 2. Broadway (New York, N.Y.) – Personal narratives. 3. Musicals – New York (State). 4. Times Square (New York, N.Y.). 5, Theater -- New York (State) -- New York – History –20th Century. I. Reich, Denise E. II. Title.
792.920   Loc PCN : 2015910829

First Edition: 2015
Printed in the United States of America

10 9 8 7 6 5 4 3 2 1

Contents

Acknowledgements	5
Overture	7

Act I: Observations

Who's Who in Ushering	16
Pay No Attention to the Elevator That Isn't There	19
Superfans	23
Herd Mentality	32
Sexism	35
Schooled on Schoolkids	37
Latecomers	42
A Fairly Large Boy	47
A Fear of Heights	49
9/13	53
Requiem for a Baby Mouse	57
The Lullaby of Broadway	60
The Ghost Light	67
Accessible Prejudice	70
Uncle Rigby	73
Broadway Kaliedoscope	77
New Year's Eve	83
Party Hearty	88
Broadway Bloopers	94
My Broadway Debut	98

Act II: Shows and Theaters

New Victory Theater	103
Shakespeare in the Park: Delacorte Theater	108
Belasco Theatre	117
Rent: Nederlander Theatre	127
Chicago: Shubert and Ambassador Theatres	131
Copenhagen: Royale Theatre	134
The Invention of Love: Lyceum Theatre	138
Def Poetry Jam: Longacre Theatre	146
Cats: Winter Garden Theatre	
Feline Rules and Regulations	151
Keith, Billy and the Brotherhood…	155
Hunting for Mistoffelees Beads	160
Are You a Cat?	164
Memory	167
Mamma Mia: Winter Garden Theatre	171
The Phantom of the Opera: Majestic Theatre	175
A Commentary on Understudies at *Phantom*	182
Wardrobe to the Rescue	183
Le Sot	186
Closing Night	190
The Pneumonia I Never Had	194
The Pneumonia I *Did* Have	199
Epilogue	204
Bibliography	208
About the Author	209

Acknowledgements

Gratitude and love to Charlene Cuomo, Meave Shelton, Michael Mantell, Beth Secrist, Greg Marlow, Carolyn Hennesy and Anna Nielsen for enthusiastically supporting this project and being beloved friends.

Grazie mille, David Belasco.

Many thanks to Tom Viola at Broadway Cares/Equity Fights AIDS.

Thank you to those at the Shubert Organization who made my time on Broadway so special, most particularly Mary Breillid; Dexter at the Belasco; Debbie at the Longacre; Francine at the Plymouth; Ronnie at the Winter Garden; Fran at the Imperial and Merida at the Lyceum; and the POTO orchestra crew: Cynthia, Gwen, Lee, Verieta and Margot.

Thanks as well to all the other friends I met along the way, and to the many on Broadway who treated me with kindness and respect, including those with whom I've lost touch, be they onstage, backstage or front of house.

I love my Mom.

Overture

I don't enjoy theater anymore. At all. It doesn't matter who is in the show, what it's about, or where it's playing. I've insulted some of my actor friends by refusing to go see their plays. I will actually buy a ticket to support them, but most of the time I won't show up. There are only a handful of very close friends who can compel me to sit through a show, and even then, even if I truly enjoy their performances, I'm always slightly uneasy about being there.

Some types of live performances are okay. Dance, for instance. I've been a dancer since I was two and a half years old, and in my mind, that splits off very neatly from theater. Cirque du Soleil? I have a lot of friends who do trapeze and aerial arts, so that works for me. Rock concerts? I'm there. A musical, however? A straight play? Please, no.

Maybe I overdosed on theater when I was younger. After spending fourteen years working on Broadway it would be a reasonable hypothesis. One *can* have too much of a good thing sometimes. Perhaps I associate live theater with work, since it *was* work for so long. . . does anyone like to go back to their office during their leisure time? I certainly don't.

My theatrical legacy comes back to me in many ways, however. As much as I tell my brain that I'm not into Broadway anymore, I'm kidding myself. It is still into me. It shows up in the way I can still quote numerous plays and musicals verbatim.

I remember music, choreography and minute set design elements from shows I saw fifteen years ago. When I read magazines and come across names I remember from Broadway, I'm immediately interested. When I hear theatrical jokes, I get the references.

I used to have a huge collection of Broadway CDs, Playbills, show jackets, cast gifts and other mementos, but several years ago, I gave almost everything away to friends. Still, theatrical souvenirs are scattered across my apartment. There are four or five signed window cards tucked away in a closet. On my bookshelf there's a pair of dance shoes that were given to me by my friend Keith, who wore them in *Cats*. There are numerous books about Broadway theaters and shows in my library, as well as a folio from a production of *The Merchant of Venice* that was personally autographed by David Belasco. Somewhere in my jewelry box there's a little tin filled with Austrian crystal Mistoffelees beads from *Cats*. There's a talisman made from more Mistoffelees crystals up on a shelf. There is even a snow globe from Broadway Cares/Equity Fights AIDS that plays "New York, New York, A Hell of a Town." It has Art Deco details from the New Amsterdam Theatre on the outside and a gaggle of Times Square buildings and show logos on the interior. At my Mom's house there's a gigantic whiskey bottle from the *Cats* Broadway set. I have some chandelier beads and a prop score from *The Phantom of the Opera* stashed somewhere.

I still get chills when I see a photo of a ghost light glowing alone on a dark stage.

Even though I don't like seeing shows anymore, I'm still a theater geek of a different sort: I love the architecture. If I find a random old theater as I'm walking down the street, I immediately grab my camera to photograph it. If I end up in a theater, whether it's being used as a live entertainment venue or a swap meet, I always spend a lot of time walking around and exploring. The more original design elements are extant, the happier I am.

I became a Broadway usher by talking my way in. I mean that quite literally. As I racked up a year of experience ushering on staff at two Off-Broadway venues, I did my homework on the theater owners who ran Broadway. I even walked into theater lobbies and asked the ticket takers who had hired them. Once I had the names I needed, I showed up at their offices, put my best foot forward, and convinced them to hire me. Afterward, I did my best to make sure they wouldn't regret it.

I was trained at a show called *Into the Whirlwind* at the Lunt-Fontanne Theatre. It was entirely in Russian and starred a number of women who were real-life survivors of Soviet gulags, prisons and persecution. They assigned me to the mezzanine, and there was frenetic activity everywhere I looked. Nobody knew where they were going, and a lot of the patrons had limited English language skills. When the show started and I was allowed to sit and rest in the gorgeous second-floor lobby, I almost melted into my chair. *What was I in for?*

The title was prophetic; I was indeed thrown right into the whirlwind. Within six months I would be working as a substitute usher all over Broadway, and within two years I would be assigned to my first permanent theater. Within four years I'd be a regular sub at a Broadway blockbuster. In eight years I'd be so disenchanted that I wouldn't enjoy seeing theater at all. In fourteen, I'd be walking away completely.

By the time I was in my late twenties I'd walked across thirteen different Broadway stages and actually performed on two of them. I'd also ushered at more than fifty different shows and worked in twenty-five Broadway theaters. It was more Broadway than many people experienced in a lifetime. During the same period of time I graduated with a four-year degree, did post-graduate work, traveled to five continents, was published in numerous magazines and books, said goodbye to my sixteen-year-old family cat, adopted two silly kittens, and lived in seven different places. I had four major operations and struggled with all manner of health issues.

While I was a college student, ushering allowed me to work and attend school full time. I gave up my weekends, but I had steady employment that didn't interfere with my class schedule. Since I was attending college on a 75% academic scholarship and my family wasn't rich, I needed the money. It was that simple. I had my own apartment, since it was actually cheaper than living in the dorms, and I had light and grocery bills to pay.

It was sometimes an arduous task: I'd get up at dawn and travel for an hour and a half to get to school, go to classes all day, walk from the Upper East Side down to the Theater District, work until almost eleven, and get home around midnight. Toward the end of my college career, when I was ushering almost every night and taking demanding classes, I was so permanently exhausted that I was almost hallucinating. The fatigue left me so drained that I wrote poetry about smiling shark heads dancing down the street and painted neon monsters. However, I still maintained an A average and I earned enough money to pay my bills in my own apartment. Did I miss out on the "college experience?" Absolutely. However, it wouldn't have meant anything to me at that time.

After I graduated with my BA from Marymount Manhattan College, I realized that majoring in Theatre Arts had been a horrific mistake. Unfortunately, it was a little too late to do much about it at that point. If I could go back in time, I'd honestly shake my seventeen-year old self and tell her to at least do a double major in Pre-Med, for God's sake. My only saving grace was that I had a BA instead of the even less commercially viable BFA. The job market was horrendous, and between the unpaid internships and the low-paying entry-level gigs, nothing I found would pay me as much or give me as many benefits as ushering did.

With that, the choice to stay on Broadway was an easy one for me. I didn't see the point of working sixty hours a week in an entry-level job in an office to earn the same income, or less, that I made as an usher. I wasn't lazy and I gave 110% to everything I did, but I did expect to have a life-work balance. Ushering afforded me the time to do things I wanted to do outside of work, and that was important. It was a survival job, not a career.

Sure, some people looked down on it, but that was their prerogative. For a time I suspected that my mother was ashamed to tell her friends what her college-educated, supposedly brilliant daughter did for a living. Once, at a party, someone actually walked away from me when I told them I worked as an usher. I really didn't care about that; I wasn't going to shape my life around someone else's expectations for me. If someone was snobby enough to dismiss me out of hand because I worked a blue-collar job, I probably didn't want to get to know them anyway. The bottom line was that ushering provided me with a higher quality of life, more money, and more free time than a so-called "professional" job would have done.

The one thing that you might notice missing from this narrative is an explanation of my vast love of theater. That's because it wasn't there. When I was growing up, one of my greatest passions was dance. I was never the bunhead that went to the studio for ten classes a week, but I consistently studied dance up through college. As a kid, when my family moved to new areas, one of the first things I usually wanted to do was find a dance studio where I could take classes. Eventually I performed in some reasonably high-level dance events, including the opening ceremonies of the 1994 World Cup at Giants Stadium.

Theater was never part of the mix. I saw shows here and there, helped write a musical in junior high and performed in school plays, but it was something that I could take or leave. I shrugged off the idea of joining the Drama Club in high school. I started doing extra and bit part work in films and TV shows when I was about sixteen, and when I got my copy of *Backstage* every week I skipped right over the listings for stage auditions.

Where did the Broadway love originate, then? Before I started my first semester of college, my mother and I decided to take in a Broadway show. I hadn't seen one since I was six years old, when we'd gone to *Annie* for my birthday. The TKTS half-price ticket booth in Times Square was offering up *Cats*, so off we went. Our seats were toward the back of the orchestra and off to the side, but they were good enough.

I don't think it is any coincidence that I was enchanted by a dance show. The entire production bewitched me, and I walked out of the theater dancing myself.

From then on, I was interested in Broadway, and particularly *Cats*. I was so obsessive about it that I hunted down cast recordings from various productions around the world: Australia, Germany, Hungary, France, Norway and Japan. I developed a crush on one of the cast members. Much of the money I earned from working went to the TKTS booth for more tickets to the show. I also discovered that other Broadway productions had student tickets and standing room. And suddenly, a new world had opened to me.

It wasn't enough to go to the show; I wanted to be a part of it. However, to be completely frank, finding a way to be in a Broadway show was not going to be easy for me. I had a lot of talents; none of them were particularly marketable on Broadway. I'd danced since I was a toddler, but Broadway choreography tended to be a bit out of my league. Since I only stood 4'11" and was, shall we say, round despite my athleticism, there wouldn't have been a lot of spots in the chorus for me anyway. I wasn't exactly going to be a Rockette. Singers didn't need to be tall, slim and leggy, but nobody was going to pay to hear my on-key, but totally unmemorable, voice on Broadway. They might have paid me to *stop* singing. I still showed up for a few Broadway chorus calls, where I dutifully executed my double pirouette and heard my 'thank you for stopping by' as I was typed out. The auditions gave me the chance to stand on a few Broadway stages and get an inside glimpse at the way chorus calls were handled, so even though I didn't have a prayer in hell of being cast, I still think they were worthwhile experiences.

What about backstage? I had neither the skills nor the interest in becoming a stagehand. When I took a stagecraft class in college I was bored stiff. I could barely sew a button so Wardrobe was out; and I didn't even know how to put on eyeliner, so a job in the Makeup department wasn't happening. I couldn't play an instrument at an advanced level, so I could scratch working in a Broadway orchestra, too.

As for the front of the house, since I looked about fourteen years old for a long time, there was no way anyone was going to allow me to be a bartender. Someone would have called Child Protective Services on the theater, I think.

My attention to detail, photographic memory, ability to deal with lots of different personalities and dogged determination probably would have made me an absolutely wonderful stage manager or dramaturge. I had no idea how to get into either of those professions, though. What was left? For me, the most plausible, and easiest, route to Broadway employment was ushering.

And so it went. I was determined to work on Broadway, and I found a way in.

If the seventeen-year-old fangirl I was had ever known that she was going to be able to go backstage at *Cats* and get paid to see so many shows, she would have fainted with joy. If she'd known that she was still going to be ushering when she was thirty, however, she might have been slightly concerned.

Three years old and in love with dance class.

Act I: Observations

Who's Who in Ushering

USHER – Let's get this one out of the way first. As the name suggests, ushers read tickets and escort patrons to their seats. They also prepare Playbills for distribution, secure theater exits at intermission and the end of the show, try to ensure that the local fire codes are met, answer questions, troubleshoot problems, try to calm down irate customers, locate lost children or their parents, assist disabled patrons and keep an eye on safety concerns around the theater. In shows where actors come into the auditorium, ushers may be directly responsible for their well-being by keeping the aisles clear, keeping guests away from them, or guarding their entrance or exit paths.

Broadway ushers are not volunteers; they're paid employees and members of the International Alliance of Theatrical Stage Employees (IATSE) union.

CHIEF – Also called the head usher, she or he is charge of the ushering staff. She or he calls the shots, assigns aisles and stations and takes care of relevant clerical duties, such as submitting the ushers' payroll to the house manager. The chief often works directly with the house managers to solve problems. As far as I know, all head ushers start out as rank-and-file and work their way up.

DIRECTOR – There may be one or several, depending on the size of the theater. The directors are the chief's first mates, so to speak. They direct patrons to the right sections, deal with problems, and sometimes act as substitute chiefs. They're often in charge during the show. The house manager and/or chief usually choose the directors.

REGULAR/PERMANENT USHER – An usher who is on permanent staff at the theater. She or he doesn't have to call in for work every week; as long as the theater is open, the job is there. Some regulars work at the same theater for decades; others bounce around. When their theaters are closed and they have to work at other venues, regular ushers tend to become regular subs.

REGULAR SUBS – Substitute ushers that stay in one place for a while, filling an empty spot in the regular roster or covering for a permanent usher who is sick, on vacation, or otherwise on a leave of absence. They usually get a lot of respect and tend to step into regular spots when they become available.

SUBS – The vagabonds who travel around Broadway and work performances for regular ushers who are out for a night or two. Some do it by choice; some do it because there's no work; some do it because they haven't climbed the ladder high enough to get a permanent house. Subs have to call the theater owners every week to get work. Sometimes they're lucky enough to get eight performances at the same place; sometimes they bounce around to numerous theaters in a single week, and sometimes work is slow and they only pick up a show here and there.

There are a lot of unrealistic stereotypes about those who work service jobs. At the top of the list, there's the pervasive misconception that service professionals lack intelligence or education. On one occasion, a patron told me that I was "really stupid," and that I'd probably "never been out of Hoboken." The irony of these statements was that I'd recently returned from a year-long stay in South Africa but I'd actually never been to Hoboken. As for the crack about intelligence, since I was a card-carrying member of Mensa as well as a university graduate, I doubt I was the stupid one in our conversational pair.

Most of the other ushers I knew were university graduates. Some had master's degrees or were in the process of earning them. Many juggled ushering with school, as I had, or with other employment. I knew ushers who were editors at major publishing houses, mid-level employees at well-known non-profit organizations and teachers. As one might expect, there were also plenty of aspiring actors, musicians and writers, some of whom booked steady work. I remember one lovely woman in her sixties who did a lot of commercials and print ads, usually playing a kindly grandmother. Another usher hosted a children's show for a major TV network. Some ushers were retirees who wanted to stay active, and they had truly intriguing life stories. At one theater there was a retired Playboy Bunny; at another there was a former Roxyette. For some ushering was a family affair, and their mothers, uncles, sisters and cousins all worked around Broadway. You had to be very careful about what you said about other ushers; you never knew if you were talking to someone's relative, partner or best friend.

Words to the wise, then: the usher you push aside or insult today might be onstage tomorrow. They might also be mixing your medication, defending you in court or writing a book you enjoy (hopefully).

Pay No Attention to the Elevator That Isn't There

Patron: *Is there an elevator I can use?*
Denise: *No, I'm sorry.*
Patron: *What's that behind you? Isn't that an elevator?*
Denise: *Um... no. Of course not.*
(Elevator doors open)

Broadway theaters are architectural marvels. If you look closely, you can find intriguing details in every house. There are the Tiffany lights on the ceiling in the Belasco. There's the Art Nouveau styling of the New Amsterdam. There are murals and chandeliers that glisten with thousands of crystals; there are secret passages and hidden levels and doors to unknown regions backstage.

The only things the designers forgot were the elevators. Back in 1905 or 1915, apparently they weren't in demand.

In the early 1980s a number of beloved historic Broadway theaters were demolished; most of the remaining houses are now landmarked as a result. However, landmark designation also comes with strict limitations on renovating or changing the structure, which means that installing elevators is, for all intents and purposes, out of the question. Every bit of space in a theater is used, so in most cases, there just isn't any place to build an elevator anyway.

As a further complication, in several of the very old theaters, there are small elevators that don't go to the seating areas. In the

Belasco Theatre, there used to be an elevator up to David Belasco's private apartment, for instance.

A similar apartment exists in the Lyceum Theatre, built in 1903. Daniel Frohman once lived there. He and his brother Charles ran the Lyceum until Charles died in the *Lusitania* sinking of 1915. According to Louis Botto's *At This Theatre*, Daniel remained in show business, but lost his money and his theaters during the Great Depression. The Lyceum's new owners allowed him to remain in his apartment for $1 a year in rent.

The next time you're in the Lyceum, turn your back to the stage and look up. You'll see what looks like a window on the left-hand side of the ceiling. It's part of the apartment, and Daniel Frohman watched performances from that vantage point. His wife was an actress, and, as legend has it, if she happened to be over-acting, Daniel would wave a handkerchief through the window to let her know.

Daniel Frohman's apartment is now occupied by the Shubert Archives, an amazing repository of delicious and fascinating theatrical memorabilia and documentation. The elevator to the apartment is still used by the Archives employees. Unfortunately, like the other old lifts, it won't help a patron in any way. It doesn't go to the seating areas and there's no way to configure it so that it does.

It's hard to convince people that there isn't an elevator in the theater when there's one right behind you. It's doubly hard when the elevator doors actually open and people saunter out. Such was the conundrum I faced at the Lyceum. The elevator doors weren't hidden, and patrons saw them as they walked upstairs. On most days of the week, I could usually placate audience members who wanted to use the elevator by claiming that it was simply a relic that was no longer in service. On Wednesday matinees, when the Shubert Archives staff came and went, it was much harder to make that fib stick. Why didn't I just tell them that the elevator went to the Archives? People tend to get annoyed when you say, "Well, yes, it works, just not for you."

The elevator was located at the junction between the mezzanine and the balcony. The Lyceum was one of those very old theaters where the two levels split off; there was no way for a patron to get from one section to the other, and they each had their own facilities. When patrons entered the theater they walked up a short flight of stairs, had their tickets checked by a director, and then either veered to the left to access the mezzanine or to the right to head up to the balcony.

The balcony was about a million flights up in the Lyceum. It was one of the steepest balconies on Broadway, and if I'm completely honest, it always made me queasy. I'm not afraid of heights, so that's saying something. I was relieved that I didn't get assigned there very often. Whenever I worked as a director on the stairs and I had to send a patron to the balcony, I almost wanted to apologize to them.

Needless to say, a lot of balcony patrons took one look at the endless flights of stairs, balked, and came straight back to me. "Isn't there an elevator?" they would ask, desperately.

"No, I'm sorry, there isn't," I would say apologetically.

Ten to one, just as I finished telling the patron that the elevator didn't exist, the doors behind me would slide open and a Shubert Archives staff member would sheepishly walk out.

"What is that, then?!" the patrons would scream. It did look, for all the world, as if I'd been lying to them.

"It doesn't go to this building," I'd try to explain. "It can't take you anywhere near the seating area. I'm sorry about that." My poor balcony patrons always looked annoyed, but they'd sigh, strap on their hiking boots and oxygen, and start the long trek up to the Heavens.

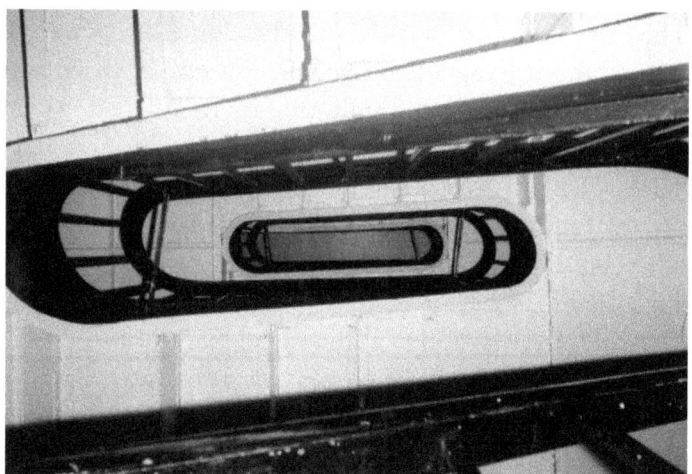

The endless staircase to the balcony of the Lyceum Theatre.

Superfans

I've never seen raw Broadway marketing data, but I can still give you a very clear cross-section of theater demographics. After you've been working a while you notice who's showing up at your theater. A lot of patrons are tourists or business travelers who are more or less ambivalent about the specific show they see. They're only staying in the city for a short period of time, they aren't really attached to any particular play or musical, and they just want to see something, *anything,* as long as it's on Broadway, to round out their New York experience.

There are patrons who don't want to be there at all, but have been dragged along by a partner or friend. Those people are easy to spot: they tend to be rude and angry, and they sometimes wander out into the lobby and text on their phones instead of watching the show.

There are always school groups that are completely indifferent. They're on a class trip, and their night on Broadway is just one of many stops on the tour itinerary for them, like the Statue of Liberty or the Museum of Natural History. At the other end of the spectrum are really enthusiastic kids. They're often aspiring actors; they know the lyrics to every Stephen Sondheim or Andrew Lloyd Webber song ever composed, appear in local community theater shows, and play Javert in the school version of *Les Misérables.* They come to New York on Drama Club trips or with their families, they are very particular with the shows they see, and they are sometimes so overwhelmed and happy to be there that they actually weep with joy.

Do New Yorkers go to Broadway shows? Maybe, maybe not. Given the high costs of Broadway tickets, a lot of locals just can't afford them. I only saw one Broadway show when I was a child because the tickets were far too expensive. My mother took me to see *Annie* just before it closed on Broadway. Buying affordable tickets to the show required my family to wait on line for hours in freezing temperatures at TKTS, the half-price ticket booth in Times Square. Even a half-price discount doesn't help much anymore, though, since the average price of a Broadway ticket is now more than $100 and hit shows charge almost $500 for some seats.

Sometimes when I was ushering I saw families or couples that obviously didn't get to go the theater very often. They were typically dressed to the nines and they always smiled ear to ear. Occasionally, they told me straight up that it was their very first Broadway show or a once in a lifetime event. Whenever I met those enthusiastic theatergoers I always felt happy to be a small part of their special night, and I went out of my way to be especially kind and accommodating to them.

There are other New Yorkers who are lucky enough to attend the theater on a regular basis with the help of heavy discounts. Some of them purchase subscriptions to theater companies that regularly produce shows on Broadway, such as the Roundabout or Manhattan Theatre Club. Some individuals who are elderly, disabled or employed in certain professions qualify for inexpensive tickets from TDF, the Theatre Development Fund. Some wait in line all day or throw their names into lotteries for the cheap standing room or standby tickets that many productions offer. In lieu of the shortcuts, some just save their pennies to devote their leisure time and income to Broadway.

And then there are the superfans, who attend the shows they love at any price.

Who are the superfans? They're the people who harbor intense attachments to specific shows, characters or actors. If they're locals they might come to the show they love every single week. If they don't live in New York they frequently make trips to the city in which they see the same production four or five times, back to back. The superfans often have message boards, websites or blogs where they expound on every detail of their Broadway experiences. Some write fan fiction about the characters or actors. They know the show better than anyone else, and they're immediately aware if a character's costume has been changed, an actor has dropped a line, or a prop has gone missing. They recognize every single performer at the stage door.

During my years on Broadway I encountered many superfans. It was usually hard for me to remember patrons, given that I interacted with so many every day, but some superfans were hard to forget.

Over at *Cats* at the Winter Garden, there was a guy who attended at least one performance every week. He always had a standing room ticket, but he often ended up sitting down front if the seats were empty. Nobody stopped him; after all those visits he was practically part of the staff. As I recall, he was so well known around the *Cats* company that he was invited to the closing night party and interviewed for at least one TV show. There were numerous other regulars at *Cats,* too. I wasn't there the night the cosplayers descended upon the Winter Garden in full feline costumes and makeup, but I was told that the ushers had to ask them to remove their wigs so the people sitting behind them could see. They were also asked to refrain from crawling around onstage at intermission. I'm not judging, I'm just reporting.

There was another very nice man who liked to bring new friends to *Cats* on a regular basis. He always gave them a typed synopsis of the plot and a complete list of characters so they'd understand what was going on. When *Cats* was in the last few months of its run, a group of fans even arranged a special party and made custom t-shirts for the cast and crew. I still have mine.

There were regulars at *The Phantom of the Opera* as well. I once met a very wealthy man who got to know his future wife at *Phantom*, proposed to her at *Phantom*, and had a *Phantom*-themed wedding. I think they also offer that option in Las Vegas, right alongside the Elvis and *RMS Titanic* rites.

Fans came to *Phantom* in costume, too. Those outfits were much less extreme than the ones I saw at *Cats*: they usually consisted of simple white masks, fedoras or capes. Once, though, a young girl came in wearing a stunning homemade replica of Christine Daaé's blue Act II dress. She was only about thirteen years old and she'd managed to sew a Victorian evening gown, down to the bustle. It was incredibly impressive. Someone really should have offered her an apprenticeship or job in Wardrobe.

I was told that some of the Rentheads down at the Nederlander often showed up dressed like their favorite characters.

A gift from Cats *fans, with original artwork by Anna-Karin Larsson.*

Spring Awakening had a really dedicated band of followers. *Wicked* once did an entire skit about their adolescent fangirls at a BC/EFA benefit show. At *Kat and the Kings*, a small contingent of fans attended so many performances that they developed responses to the dialogue, a la *The Rocky Horror Show*.

My mother had a co-worker who saw *Les Misérables* on a regular basis. He was a psychologist, and he used *Les Mis* in his therapy program for wounded veterans. In the show, a group of students and activists revolt against the French government. Only one, a young man named Marius, survives the battle. In the song "Empty Chairs at Empty Tables," he laments the loss of his friends and expresses his guilt and disbelief at the fact that he is still alive. This psychologist used the song and the character of Marius as prompts for discussions about survivors' guilt with his patients, who had seen many of their fellow soldiers die in Vietnam, Iraq or Afghanistan.

Certain performers had active fan clubs. Some of the understudies had devotees who showed up every time they went on. I remember one woman at *Jekyll & Hyde* who came to seemingly all of Robert Evan's performances. She'd march purposefully down the aisle in her *Jekyll & Hyde* show jacket and go right to her seat in the front row. After a while none of us bothered her; we recognized her and knew that she knew where she was going.

I couldn't and wouldn't judge any of this, especially since I'd embarrassed myself crushing on various Broadway performers and hanging out at stage doors in the past (if you've ever played Mistoffelees in *Cats* on Broadway, please accept my apologies at this time). If we think about it, we've probably all been fans of something or other. Even if we don't reach the point of obsession, our lives are still enriched by the things we love. Maybe it's *Doctor Who*. It could be Harry Potter. Perhaps it's a football, hockey or baseball team. My teenage loves were Guns N' Roses, the novel *The Vampire Lestat* and, later on, *Cats*, which are an unlikely trio. Every now and then I'll read a story of someone who was saved from suicide or helped through depression by something that resonated with them in a book they read or a song they heard. It's what art is supposed to do: grab our hearts and hang on. When it comes down to it, healthy doses of mania and passion probably help most of us get through the day.

The vast majority of the superfans I met on Broadway were kind, lovely people. A few, however, made me very uneasy, and as a rule I stayed away from them as much as possible. Sometimes the line between affectionate zeal and disturbing obsession was too blurred for comfort. If a superfan set off my Spidey Sense for any reason while I was working, I'd keep an eye on them and ask my colleagues to do the same. If I *really* felt that they were too obsessive or fixated, I'd let the house manager know about it, just to be on the safe side. On one occasion, a fan that had exhibited very bizarre behavior in the past tried to kiss up to a chorus dancer I knew. As soon as I found out about it, I immediately took my friend aside and warned him to be careful.

That wasn't unusual, for what it's worth. Broadway staff, both front and back of house, tend to be fiercely protective of the actors. They do whatever they can to keep the performers safe. When I was working, I was frequently grilled about performers' sexual orientations, places of residence or marital status. Some people asked where the actors went after the show or which routes they took home. My stock answer was to smile, shrug and say "I'm sorry, I just don't know."

Even seemingly innocent questions came with ulterior motives, and you had to be very careful when dealing with them. For instance, if I were ever asked if I liked a particular performer, I knew to tread very, very lightly. There were only two appropriate answers, regardless of how I really felt: "Yes, s/he is great," and "Oh, I haven't seen him/her perform yet." Why? For one thing, we obviously couldn't bash the show for which we worked. For another, we never knew if a friend or family member of the actor in question was trolling us. It actually happened on occasion.

If someone asked me how to meet a performer, I could let

them know where the stage door was located. That information was freely shared because fans were expected to congregate there. I always cautioned that the actors might or might not sign autographs or stop to say hello, and that nobody could make any promises about it. If an audience member wanted to know how long a particular actor had been with the show, I could share that, too. If they asked who was playing a specific character at that performance, I was happy to tell them. In general, though, those were the only details I would provide about the actors, regardless of what I actually knew. If it wasn't listed in the Playbill, it wasn't for me to disclose. It was that simple. I wasn't there to gossip about the performers. None of the Powers That Be set down any explicit rules about this, but we all exercised common sense and watched what we said.

Such vigilance might sound extreme, but it was necessary: a handful of superfans turned out to be stalkers. The good news was that security and management at every theater took threats against the cast or crew very seriously. If a performer mentioned that they were uncomfortable, or if a superfan's behavior became too erratic or persistent, it was scrutinized and responded to accordingly. Everyone took precautions to try to keep the actors safe.

At one production I worked, a woman was obsessed with a musician in the orchestra pit. She was completely deranged, and she wrote several bizarre letters to the man in which she made frightening comments about his wife and child. Consequently, she was banned from the theater and asked to stay away from the musician. I think a formal restraining order might have actually been involved. Her photo was posted in the ushers' room and we were asked to alert security or management immediately if we saw her. Inevitably, she couldn't bear to stay away, returned to the theater, and was arrested on the spot.

Most of the time we didn't see that level of extremism, though. Squabbles did break out in fan groups, but they fought amongst themselves, not with the theater staff. However, some fans seemed to harbor irrational hostility toward performers' friends and loved ones.

I felt the force of fan Haterade myself one evening when I stopped in at the Palace Theatre to see Hugh Panaro perform in the musical *Lestat*. I'd long been a fan of the first three books of Anne Rice's Vampire Chronicles, and I was eager to see how they'd been adapted to the stage. In addition, I liked Hugh Panaro. I'd started working as a regular at *Phantom* during one of his runs as the title character, and I'd had a chance to talk to him at a few cast parties. He was one of the nicest performers I'd ever met, so I stuck around after *Lestat* to say hello to him and offer congratulations on his new show.

There was a fairly large throng of people at the stage door and metal barricades had been set up to give the performers a clear getaway path. When Hugh appeared I stood back and watched as he worked his way down the fence, posed for photos, talked to fans and signed autographs. When he was done, he turned to me and gave me a big hug. We talked for a few moments, he asked about life over at *Phantom*, and we said goodbye with a smile.

Meeting Hugh Panaro at a Phantom *party. No superfans were angered in the taking of this photo.*

As I turned to leave, I noticed that several of the fangirls at the barricade were glaring at me. None of them said anything and none of them approached me, but their demeanor was enough to make me very ill at ease.

Apparently, even being a very casual acquaintance of a performer can be a hazardous occupation. It pisses off the superfans.

Herd Mentality

Denise: Ladies and Gentlemen, we have three exits. If you're waiting over here, please exit through the box.
Patron: I'm going this way.
Denise: Yes, but your wait will be twice as long. And these two different staircases actually meet at the lobby...
Patron: I'm staying here, young lady!
Denise: (sigh) Fine.

There are those who claim that humanity has a herd mentality. Everyone mindlessly follows the person in front of them without stopping to consider where they're going. If you ever want to see this concept in action, watch the crowd at the end of a Broadway show.

Here's the basic rule when you're trying to leave after a performance: if a door is open and the ushers are freely allowing patrons to walk through, it's safe to say that it's an exit you can use. If the curtain or door is closed, or if an usher is standing in front of it, presume that you can't go that way. The ushers aren't trying to obstruct your access to those exits because they're evil bitches; they just don't want you ending up on a fire escape instead of the street.

There are usually more ways to get out of a theater than there were to go in, however. After the final curtain you might discover that all the doors across the orchestra level are flung wide open, or you might be directed to exit through a staircase by the boxes. The ushers and managers try to ensure that everyone has safe, fast paths for egress.

Here's the curious thing, though: most people don't try to find the quickest or easiest way out. They zero in on one particular exit, even if it's not the closest one, and huddle with the thousand other patrons who are trying to leave that way. They just follow the person in front of them and don't bother to look around. Consequently, there will often be two exits that are completely empty, while twenty feet away, scores of people are jostling to leave via the third.

I always tried to combat this by directing people to use all the exits, to take the stairs they hadn't noticed, or to walk across the rows of seats to bypass the crowds and make use of all the open orchestra doors. I tended to be somewhat zealous about it, and as a result, my sections usually tended to clear out quickly. At one theater, the chief called me "the sweeper."

Let's be honest: it was somewhat self-serving, because I wanted to go home. I couldn't leave until my section was clear. The faster that happened, the faster I could get out of there. However, I also really *was* trying to deliver good customer service. I figured that the patrons might be happier if they only spent five minutes exiting as opposed to fifteen. I don't know anyone who really enjoys trudging along through a slow-moving crowd, and there's no reason to wait for Exit A when Exits B and C are totally open.

What was always surprising to me was the way some people reacted to being told there was an alternative exit available. They'd fix me with icy stares and coldly inform me, "I'm going this way." This happened even when I tried to explain that the two staircases actually went to the exact same place in the lobby, so they didn't have to wait for the one that was overcrowded. It was as though they thought I was trying to deliberately mislead them. That sounds melodramatic, perhaps, but judging from the reactions I got, some people genuinely seemed to believe that I had some nefarious intention when I tried to show them a different way out.

On some nights things were impossible, everyone refused to listen, and by the time we left the theater the ghost light had already been wheeled onstage and turned on. As we walked through the lobby we'd hear people complaining about how long it had taken them to exit, and how they couldn't believe the theater didn't have more doors. And then we'd laugh, cry and shake our heads as we went off to get late dinner.

Sexism

Universal Truth: if a male and female usher are standing together, a patron in need of assistance will always approach the male employee. If two women or two men are standing together, they will ask the usher who is white. If both ushers are of the same race and gender, the patron will ask the one who is younger or thinner. It almost always works that way. People might think that sexism and ageism are dead, but when you work in a theater, you learn that's not the case at all.

At *Phantom*, patrons would sometimes completely ignore instructions I'd given them, only to comply immediately when a male colleague told them the exact same thing two seconds later. Likewise, there were times when I'd give them information and they'd look to a male usher for confirmation. They naturally thought that the guy standing next to me was my supervisor, even if he was a sub who had only been working for two weeks.

I also had to contend with patrons who tried to be overly familiar with me. For some reason, both men and women often felt they had the right to grab me, put their arms around my shoulders or lean in close to ask questions. They absolutely never did the same to my male colleagues, and they were always very offended when I politely dislodged their hands, wriggled out of their grasp, and backed up.

At some shows I was groped. I sometimes had to contend with very grabby old men who inexplicably thought that I was going to be overjoyed by their attentions. I finally started putting my hand up in a "stop" gesture and stepping back when these octopus-like patrons approached me and extended their tentacles. I learned to tell them straight out, "I'll be happy to help you, but please don't touch me." Outside of the theater, I would have told them to get the hell away from me and probably would have considered kicking them in the shins; at work I had to find ways to deal with it professionally and peacefully.

It still irks me that I *had* to deal with it, though.

On other occasions male patrons referred to me in ways that were clearly meant to be insulting, such as "girl." At *Phantom* one evening, I tried to stop a couple from taking their drinks to their seats. They told me that "my supervisor" behind the bar had told them it was fine. Knowing that none of my supervisors happened to work behind a bar, I politely told the couple that regardless of what the bartender had told them, he wasn't in charge, and they couldn't take their drinks in. The man shook his finger in my face and snapped, "You need to talk to your boss, and you have a lot to learn, young lady."

Every now and then I even encountered patrons who thought that I was going to babysit their children during the show. They'd bring them to wherever I was stationed and say, "This nice lady will watch you." Again, I doubt they would have done the same with a male usher. They were always very disgruntled when I told them that I couldn't babysit and that their children needed to stay with them, in their immediate vicinity, at all times.

And so on. And so forth. Ad nauseam.

Can I say one more thing about this issue? There's no such thing as an usherette. "Ette" is a diminutive, and female ushers aren't lesser beings. Both men and women are ushers, plain and simple.

Schooled on Schoolkids

There were three words I always dreaded hearing when I was ushering: "We're all together." The phrase was usually uttered by the leader of a large party of schoolchildren or a tour group, none of whom intended to show us their tickets or sit in the correct seats.

Cats, Phantom, Les Misérables and *Miss Saigon* all attracted a lot of kids; at some Wednesday matinees students occupied more than half the seats in the building. Many productions, especially the large musicals, had full educational outreach programs with study guides, workbooks, plot summaries, fact sheets, and other material to supplement teachers' own preparations. Sometimes students who attended matinees were able to stick around after the performance for question-and-answer sessions with the actors or stage managers.

For some schools Broadway was just another field trip; for others, it was the highlight of the academic year. Many student groups came from the New York/New Jersey/Connecticut tri-state area; others traveled longer distances. They changed with the seasons. In the summer the day camps came in. At Thanksgiving, the big musicals always got the members of the high school marching bands and color guards that performed in the Macy's Thanksgiving Day Parade. The kids usually proudly wore their red parade "cast member" jackets and carried special duffel bags with the Macy's logo.

Unfortunately, many student groups failed to understand that they didn't actually have the entire theater to themselves, so they really couldn't sit wherever they pleased. Dealing with this could be an absolute nightmare. At Wednesday matinees we often had four or five different groups from different schools doing kangaroo hops around the mezzanine. And of course, when they ended up in someone else's seats, it became a nightmare when those ticket holders actually showed up. We often spent the entire walk-in kicking kids out of seats they didn't have. It was enough to reduce some ushers to tears.

Even worse, sometimes the kids didn't behave during the show, but spent the entire time twittering and hissing like a pack of locusts. *Les Misérables* in particular tended to make teens and 'tweens antsy because it was so long, had so many quiet moments, and dealt with a period of history that most of them didn't know very much about. I'd wager that many of them had heard about the 1789 French Revolution and Napoleon in school, but hadn't learned anything about France in the mid-1800s. As far as I remember from my own school days, the World History curriculum covered exactly six topics about France: Louis XIV, the 1789 French Revolution, Napoleon, the Dreyfus Affair, and France's involvement in WWI and WWII. And I supposedly went to good schools. Point being, for many students, there wasn't anything familiar in *Les Misérables*. For what it's worth, the original production of *Les Mis* offered an amazing teacher's guide to combat this obstacle and prepare young people for the show. I read it. It was good. The catch was whether the teachers actually used it.

Even if they understood the history, a lot of students were stymied by the show's running time. *Les Mis* originally clocked in at three hours and fifteen minutes. At some point toward the end of its first Broadway run it was edited down slightly, but even then, it was still only a hair away from the three-hour mark. It was too long for some kids to handle. Pity, because it's an incredible show.

At *Miss Saigon,* which played in the huge Broadway Theatre, the back of the mezzanine was sometimes closed during matinees and concealed with a velvet curtain. The ushers working upstairs always had to watch the curtain, because students could and would try to go behind it to make out.

Some groups were so badly behaved that they didn't even make it through the performance; security escorted them out. On occasion, they managed to distract the actors. I heard about an incident at *Les Misérables* where kids in the audience threw Skittles at the actress playing Fantine as she tried to sing "I Dreamed a Dream." She was eventually so rattled that she went offstage in tears, and the show was temporarily stopped while the offending school group was removed.

On other days the disruptions didn't reach such an extreme level, but we still spent most of intermission fielding complaints, apologizing to the justifiably annoyed patrons who were sitting near the students; sending said patrons to the house manager to be relocated; warning the school groups to stop talking; and pleading with the teachers to at least *try* to control their charges. security would often appear at intermission on these chaotic days to warn the students that if they continued to behave badly they would be escorted from the theater.

We could usually tell how the afternoon was going to go by the way the teachers interacted with us. If a group's adult chaperones were rude to the ushers, the young people tended to follow the example that had been set. If the teachers didn't sit with the students, but went off on their own to cluster together in their own little social group, we knew we were in trouble.

In contrast, when the teachers sat on the ends of each row and took the time to directly supervise and guide their kids, there weren't nearly as many issues. Many students had never been to a Broadway show before, and they truly didn't know how they were supposed to behave. Some teachers recognized this and took pains to educate their kids on theater etiquette. Best of all, in this respect, were the drama and English teachers who handpicked the students who attended, made them dress up, admonished them on proper behavior in the theater, and knew to hand over all the tickets in one pack. We never heard a peep from those students.

At a revival of August Wilson's drama *Ma Rainey's Black Bottom* at the Royale Theatre, the poor conduct of students in attendance completely destroyed a few performances. We had large numbers of high schoolers at every matinee, and they behaved abominably. At one show, the kids were so raucous during Charles Dutton's dramatic monologue that he refused to come out at curtain call.

The production staff blamed us, even though we'd done everything possible to calm the kids down. Shortly thereafter, the stage manager gathered us for a meeting in the back of the orchestra. We attended reluctantly; everyone was annoyed and indignant about being blamed for the melee. We didn't like it when audience members interfered with the show any more than the backstage contingent did.

Truthfully, we'd done all we could. We'd called security and the house manager, because the situation had been well above our heads. The ushers hadn't had any clout with those students; they'd known we could neither fail them nor call their parents. Their teachers hadn't backed us up. Thus, the kids hadn't felt any compunction to listen to a single word we said to them. In addition, we had been severely outnumbered. When there were about ten of us versus several hundred kids, who did they *think* was going to win?

During the show, there was no way we could stop so many kids from talking. When one or two students were noisy, standing next to them or quietly asking them to stop sometimes solved the problem, if they respected the ushers enough to listen and comply. If a handful of kids were antsy, talking to their teachers at intermission sometimes helped, but only if they were cooperative and willing to take responsibility for their students' conduct. When an entire section was out of control, though, our attempts to intervene always proved futile. The only effective recourse we had was to let security and the house manager know about it. Even security's options were limited; most of the time they had to wait until intermission to kick the group out. Removing a hundred angry kids during the performance could be far more disruptive than letting them stay, so it usually only happened if things had truly gone nuclear.

My colleague Jamie slumped indolently against the standing room wall as we listened to the stage manager's lecture.

"You need to be listening," she admonished us.

"I *am* listening," said Jamie.

"Your body language says otherwise," the stage manager retorted.

"What do you want us to *do*, exactly?" someone asked.

The question seemed to catch the stage manager off guard. "Well," she stammered, "Keep doing what you're doing. . . I guess." She was lecturing us because we were an easy target, but she didn't even know what she expected us to do to stop the problem. The rest of the discussion was much more proactive and respectful on both sides.

At the next matinee the kids were on their best behavior. Why? The teachers stepped up. The students were brought to us in manageable groups, and they'd apparently really been warned about behaving during the performance. There were many more adult chaperones accompanying them, as well. In addition, we had extra security. Nobody disrupted the monologue, the stage managers were pleased, our relationship with the backstage contingent improved greatly, and the blame game stopped.

The school groups are still going to *Phantom* and other shows in force. *Les Misérables* is back; I'm sure there are teenagers sleeping and texting through "On My Own" even as I write this.

Latecomers

"I'll move if someone comes in." Along with "we're all together," this is a phrase that ushers hate to hear. I know I did when I was working. It generally comes from a person who has hopped from their reserved seat to a vacant one and is resisting returning to their original place.

At many shows, audience members try to sneak into other seats as soon as the lights go down; we see their hunched-over forms scurrying down the stairs and aisles in the dark, like roaches. Some standing room patrons will plunk themselves into empty seats as soon as the curtain goes up. In other cases, people attempt to move up before the show starts.

When I saw this, I really had no choice but to go after the patrons and send them back to their original seats. I often took a lot of verbal abuse in the process or had to listen to long debates.

I know, I know. It's hard to see an empty seat, especially in an enticing area, and hear an usher tell you that it's unavailable. Whenever I'm at a show I surely appreciate the opportunity to spread out a little. I can especially understand this if you have a standing room ticket and you're facing the prospect of spending close to three hours on your feet. It's easy to think of an usher who is blocking you from moving up as a little person on a power trip; numerous patrons who were angry that I wouldn't let them relocate certainly told me as much.

However, the ushers aren't denying you the chance to move because they're horrible trolls. Really. They are just trying to keep the show from being disrupted as much as possible. In other words, they're trying to ensure that everyone, including you, has a great experience at the performance.

See, there's a high probability that someone has already purchased the seats you want. Said patrons are most likely going to come in late. If the seats are empty, the usher can quickly throw the latecomers in. It's a disruption, but a minor one. If people have moved into those seats, however, it's a problem. The usher then has to shine her flashlight down the row, check everyone's tickets, kick out the people who don't belong there, and finally seat the latecomers. . . who, by the way, have been standing in the aisle, blocking others' view of the show, during this entire exchange. After that the usher has to reseat the errant party who moved up and hope that nobody has moved into *their* seats. This assumes everything goes smoothly and the "relocated guests" cooperate and don't try something cute, such as pretending they can't hear the usher when she asks for their tickets. Just so you know, that never works; it just earns you a nice conversation with security.

At the end of the day it's a horrendous mess, it disturbs everyone, and it can be avoided if you simply keep your butts in the seats to which you're assigned. Or, at the very least, use your brains and think critically about it. Common sense says not to plunk yourselves down into those two empty seats that are dead center in an otherwise totally occupied row. Really, guys, do you *think* those are going to remain empty?

This even holds true if there's a huge gaping section of empty seats. Especially then. I always cringed when I saw those sections, because it often meant that a huge group was running late. I worked at some performances where several hundred people came in halfway through Act I. Let me tell you, friends, those situations were horrible for everyone.

It would be great if everyone arrived on time, but one has to be realistic: it's New York. Things happen. Buses get caught in traffic, they get lost, they discover that they can't park in front of the theater and they have trouble finding places to discharge their passengers. Subways stop in the tunnels or don't come at all.

Tourists can't figure out the lay of the land. There are a thousand plausible reasons why a patron who means well and ostensibly leaves enough travel time might not make it to the theater by curtain. I was late to a show once when I was in London because I walked the wrong way from the Tube station and got hopelessly lost. I didn't make it to the theater until well after curtain time.

Given all of the above, I tried to be sympathetic toward latecomers. The only time they became annoying was when they took out their frustrations on me. Hey, I understood that they were upset at missing part of the show. I comprehended that whatever held them up had probably been stressful, and that their anxiety levels were still high. However, that wasn't my fault. *I* hadn't made them late.

There are usually specific cues in both straight plays and musicals when ushers are allowed to seat patrons. At musicals the seating cues tend to be either during the overture or at the ends of songs, while everyone is applauding. At some productions there are also complete no-fly zones during the performance when people aren't even allowed to go to their seats if they are returning from the bathroom and don't need our help. At *Phantom*, for example, nobody comes in during "Music of the Night," period.

I always tried to hold people at the top of the aisle or on the side of the orchestra so they could watch the show while they were waiting to be seated. It wasn't always possible, though, and every production had its own policies on latecomers. At *Copenhagen* they had to sit in the back row until intermission. At *Miss Saigon, Blast, Bombay Dreams* and *Les Misérables,* latecomers couldn't go into the auditorium at all until the show was about twenty minutes in; in the meantime they had to watch the performance on the television screens in the lobby. I also worked at a handful of shows that didn't admit latecomers at all. If you weren't there by the time the curtain went up you were out of luck.

Some performers worked patron lateness into their shows. The original *Blue Man Group* off-Broadway, which I saw a few times, had the very best response to this: they played a loud song, rang sirens and showed the latecomers on a TV screen as they entered. At *Master Class*, the actress playing Maria Callas directly scorned them. John Legiuzamo, during his one-man show, *Sexaholix*, stopped, stared at the latecomers and offered up a very sarcastic "Hey, thanks for coming." For the most part, though, seating latecomers was a non-event. My goal was always to whisk them to their seats as quickly and quietly as possible.

    I often encountered latecomers who were completely put upon to learn that they had to wait to be seated. They would rail on me, telling me they wanted to be seated *right now*, and huff and puff when I told them it wouldn't be possible. They apparently thought that I was holding them back for my own personal amusement. In fact, I was following the strict regulations I'd been given by my house manager and the production staff and trying to minimize the disruption for the rest of the audience and cast. Lesson of the day: one of the fastest ways for a Broadway usher to piss off stage management and upset the creative team is to ignore the seating cues.

    Keeping to the cues was a challenge when so many guests were uncooperative. Some of them had actual temper tantrums when they heard that they would have to wait a few minutes before going to their seats. I remember a man at *The Graduate* who was so livid about it that he threw his ticket in my face. He carried on so much that I halfway expected him to stomp his feet and prostrate himself on the carpet like a toddler.

    At *The Invention of Love* we held people in the back of the orchestra for late seating. At the very last performance there was a latecomer who decided that I needed to explain every single aspect of the show to him: who was onstage, what was happening, and what he had missed. You really can't hold conversations, much less give someone a complete synopsis of the show, when you're two feet away from seated patrons who will be disturbed by the noise. I politely explained that I couldn't keep talking to him and walked away.

    Another group of latecomers came in, and I asked them to

wait in the back for the seating cue. The man stormed over to me and ranted about the fact that I had said two words to the other patrons, when I'd told him that I couldn't explain the show to him.

It was the final day of a very exhausting, stressful run, I wasn't in the mood to deal with any more rude patrons, and this guy had just stepped on my last nerve. I struggled to keep my temper in check, snapped "Sir, it's not my responsibility to explain the show to you," and walked away. I switched aisles with one of my colleagues so I wouldn't have to be near the man again. The usher who took my place was a large, strapping fellow, and I noticed that my disgruntled latecomer didn't even attempt to get a show summary from him. I wasn't surprised.

A Fairly Large Boy

One night during the walk-in at *Phantom*, a frantic man approached me. He asked me if I'd seen a "fairly large boy" walking by. I wasn't much help. There were over sixteen hundred people in the theater on a busy night at *Phantom*, including children both large and small. Since I had thirty minutes to seat about three hundred of them, I wasn't paying much attention to faces.

Here's a clue: asking an usher if they have seen your wife or friend is usually a pointless exercise. And no, it doesn't really matter if you tell us they're blonde or handsome or whatnot. We're dealing with hundreds of people in a very short period of time, and one face fades into the next. The only real exception to this is if there's something extremely unforgettable about your lost loved one's appearance; say, they have a rainbow Mohawk or they're wearing a space suit.

I sent the man to the house manager and security to report the lost child. We didn't seem to have much information to go on, and the father's answers to our questions were very vague. Was the child autistic? No. Did he have any developmental disabilities? No. What did he look like? White, blond and "fairly large." How old was he? Was that question answered?

Chaos reigned for the next ten or fifteen minutes. security was alerted. Someone watched the front door. Theater staff searched for the elusive child, but he was nowhere to be found. I personally began to worry that he'd left the theater, either on his own or in the company of an unsavory person, to wander the streets of New York. The boy's grandmother was in tears and kept crying, "I've lost my grandchild. I've lost him!" The father was also visibly upset.

Eventually, the boy was located in one of the lounges, unhurt, unruffled, and happy as a clam. The reason nobody had found him earlier was because he happened to be a six-foot-three, smart aleck sixteen year old. They hadn't mentioned that.

A Fear of Heights

When a patron approached me during walk-in or intermission I was usually expecting them to ask one of two things: "Where's the bathroom?" or "I hate my seat. What can you do about it?"

Patrons yelled at me over the seating arrangements all the time. I suppose that when someone's frustrated, it's easiest to take it out on the nearest person who cannot fight back. In most cases, that was me.

Sometimes people made requests that were beyond absurd. Once someone asked me, in all seriousness, if I could take away one of the banisters in the mezzanine. *Sure, let me grab my blowtorch and saw, I'll get right on it.* Patrons were angry with me because their seats were too close to the stage, too far away, too central, too far to the side, too high up or too low. Nobody ever seemed to understand that I hadn't assigned their seating locations. I didn't work at the box office, TKTS or Telecharge. I just read the tickets and directed them accordingly.

Every now and then we did have people who had legitimate issues with their seating, and I always tried to help them where, when and if I could. If someone was sitting next to a person with body odor or excessive perfume, for example, I empathized completely. My ability to offer direct assistance was usually limited, however. I generally had to send them off to the house manager.

Quite a few patrons turned out to be afraid of heights. On more than one occasion these acrophobics didn't even have to tell us; when they completely broke down in terror in the middle of the balcony it was painfully obvious to all.

On one memorable night when I was working the mezzanine at *Phantom* with my friend Sheila, a woman stomped up the staircase. She was roughly hauling a teenage boy behind her. The boy was in full-blown hysterics; he was frantically flailing, crying, and struggling to get away. As the woman dragged him up the stairs by one arm, he kicked his feet, pulled backward and screamed.

Sheila jumped right into the fray: "Stop that right now!" There wasn't any time to be gracious about it; we were dealing with an emergency. The woman was being downright horrible to her son, and in the process she was endangering every single person on the staircase. If either she or the boy had fallen backward during their struggle, they would have tumbled down the steps and severely injured themselves or others.

Even though the woman immediately stopped yanking the boy's arm when Sheila told her to stop, the scene was still horrific. The boy sobbed, the mother yelled, and the father and another child stood ineffectively to the side and stayed out of it.

It turned out that the kid was absolutely terrified of heights and didn't want to go to his seat in the mezzanine. The mother was trying to force him into it. She thought he was faking his terror so he could avoid seeing the show. Sheila and I disagreed. The boy was shaking, crying, and having a full-on panic attack. He kept spluttering, "You knew I couldn't do this. You *knew!*" which brought that point home even more.

We sent the father off to speak to the house manager, and two places downstairs were located for the boy and his dad. The mother and the other sibling were sent up to their original seats in the back of the mezzanine. I was honestly glad that the boy got away from that dreadful woman for at least a few hours.

It certainly wasn't the only time we dealt with intense acrophobia at the theater. In another instance at *Phantom*, a woman climbed all the way to her seat in row L – that's the very top of the mezzanine – without incident. Unfortunately, she then looked back toward the stage, realized how far up she was, and completely melted down. She was so overwhelmed and terrified that she cowered behind the last row of seats and cried. It took several ushers walking in front of her, behind her and beside her to coax her back down to the mezzanine landing so she could be relocated. She crawled down the stairs on her hands and knees, sobbing.

Why would you buy a mezzanine ticket if you were afraid of heights? I give people the benefit of the doubt on this one. Price is an issue. Broadway tickets have become horrifyingly expensive, and if the only affordable section happens to be the balcony or rear mezzanine, that's where you go. If a show is hot and tickets are hard to come by, those might be the only sections available. I also really think that sometimes when customers buy their tickets, they just don't realize how far up they're going to be. When you hear that you're in the eighth row it sounds all right, until you get to the theater and realize that the eighth row is up a sharp incline.

It doesn't help that the seating configurations and architecture at every theater differ, too. That eighth row might be feasible at one theater and completely frightening at another. A positive experience at one house doesn't indicate what you're in for at another. Some upper levels, like the mezzanine at the Winter Garden Theatre, are very gently raked. I don't recall ever hearing a single complaint about the mezzanine height at the Winter Garden. Other mezzanines and balconies are so steep that they resemble the Hillary Step on Mount Everest.

In particular, the balconies at some of the oldest theaters can be really, really scary. At a few places, like the Lyceum, I honestly felt as though I were walking up and down a ladder when I traversed the balcony. It was really that steep, and even though I had no fear of heights, it made me dizzy. I hated late seating there, because it meant that I had to navigate those steps myself.

It isn't always possible to find a satisfactory solution for everyone on this issue, unfortunately. There really isn't any way to make a balcony level in a theater that isn't high above the ground. There isn't any way to ensure that every patron will be okay with heights. Acrophobia is a problem that Broadway ushers and customers will be handling now and forever, to quote *Cats*.

9/13

On September 13, 2001, I got on the bus to go to work. I was dressed in black, as per usual, and I had an American flag ribbon on my shirt.

After the attacks on the World Trade Center, Broadway theaters stayed closed for three performances: the evening show on Tuesday, September 11 and both matinee and evening on Wednesday, September 12. On Thursday all productions resumed performances.

The only people on the express bus with me were the driver and one of the first responders. A lot of businesses were still closed, and nobody who lived in the Tri-State area was going into Manhattan unless they absolutely, positively had to do so. As we drove through midtown, everyone was quiet. We didn't need to talk about what had happened; we'd all witnessed it.

Since I worked nights, I'd been home and sleeping when the first plane hit the Twin Towers. A frantic phone call from my aunt had woken me up. Our apartment was several miles due north of the World Trade Center, and I could see the Towers from my bedroom windows. I'd spent the day numbly looking out those windows at the smoke billowing from the buildings and fielding calls from concerned out-of-town friends and relatives.

My mother, who worked in the Village, came home on 9/11 with ashes in her hair. It could have been far worse. She'd originally planned to shop in the mall below the World Trade Center that morning, which would have put her at Ground Zero at a very bad time. Thankfully, she'd changed her mind and gone straight to work, further uptown, instead.

The Theater District was silent and calm, and heavy smoke hung over the deserted streets. When I alit from the bus I nearly gagged; the stench in the air went right down my throat. It was an indescribable mix of fuel, chemicals, burning flesh and smoke. I know I will never forget it. Neither will anyone else, I'd imagine. If you talk to any New Yorker who was in town on 9/11, that stench is probably one the first things they'll mention to you. I've heard some people describe it as the smell of death; that's very accurate, in my opinion. It lingered around Times Square, constantly reminding all of us of what had occurred downtown.

I was working at the Cort Theatre at *If You Ever Leave Me. . . I'm Coming With You*, a comedic play written and performed by the husband and wife team of Joseph Bologna and Renée Taylor.

The house manager immediately called a meeting with the staff. We gathered in a circle, solemn and quiet. There was nothing to say. Some of us had experienced 9/11 more directly than others, but we were all numb and horrified. My friend Sheila, who was also steady at the Cort at the time, worked downtown during the day. Just as my mother, she'd had to run for her life. The house manager stared back, as shocked as the rest of us, and then cleared his throat and told us about the security measures they were adding to the theater. Security on Broadway was already tight; now it was going to be Fort Knox.

I don't remember what the count was that evening, but I'd be surprised if we had more than a hundred people. Who went to see a Broadway comedy three days after a national disaster? Well, for one thing, there were a lot of tourists around. The airports were still closed, so anyone who was in the city on vacation or business was essentially stuck there for the time being. There were also many people who lived in Hell's Kitchen or the Garment District and couldn't go anywhere. Whatever the reason for their presence, the patrons who visited our show on September 13 simply wanted to escape reality for a few hours and distract themselves from the disaster that was still haunting every heart, dominating every television channel and poisoning the air outside.

Our show's opening montage had originally concluded with an explosion. It goes without saying that the production team had hastily excised that particular sound effect. Instead, Renée Taylor and Joseph Bologna walked onstage together, broke the fourth wall and directly addressed the audience.

They knew it was hard to judge what was appropriate to do during a national tragedy, they said, but their job was to make people laugh. They hoped that they could temporarily take everyone's mind off the horror downtown. The small audience weakly applauded. By the end of the performance some of them were chuckling, and there might even have been a laugh or two. It was a needed respite from the death and destruction outside.

It was, however, a brief respite. A number of Broadway shows closed the next Sunday due to the sudden, drastic drop-off in ticket sales, and mine was one of them. There was no closing party; there was neither a sense of completion nor cause for celebration.

When I called for sub assignments, my boss, Erin, told me apologetically, "I don't have a single show for you." With so many theaters dark, work was hard to come by. I ended up filing for unemployment and staying on it for over a month. Thankfully, they waived the waiting week so we started getting our benefits right away.

In a way I was grateful. Given what had happened, I didn't really want to go outside. Without a show I didn't have to. I could sit in the apartment and try to process it all. Of course, if I looked out the window I could still see smoke hanging ominously over lower Manhattan.

Broadway eventually bounced back. By mid-October I was scraping up a few performances every week, and by November I was working steadily again. 9/11 hung over our heads for a very long time, however. Although none of us really discussed it, I think that most of the house staff was edgy. Whenever I saw an unattended backpack or purse on a chair, I immediately called security. I looked more closely at the people who attended the shows and paid special attention if they seemed to be studying the theater's structure more intently than normal. In the past I would have chalked up these people as theater enthusiasts, but in light of the recent tragedy, I suspected them all of having ulterior motives.

That heightened sense of suspicion never really went away. Even in my current line of work, even now, fourteen years later, I am usually the first to call security when I see someone acting even slightly erratically. I'm the first to report unattended parcels; the first to keep an eye on people who ask too many questions about the building layout. Enhanced vigilance and a touch of paranoia are what I carried from 9/11.

Requiem for a Baby Mouse

Serrated Playbill spines. Small shadows along the walls. A gray flash zipping between the seats. Chewed boxes. The theater mice made their presence known in ways large and small.

This isn't a commentary on the cleanliness of the theaters, either. There's a frequently quoted statistic that in New York City there are three or four rats for every human. If you walk down the streets of Manhattan or take a subway, you won't doubt this figure in the least. When I was bored while I was waiting for a train underground, one of my favorite games was to study the tracks and play Spot the Rat. It doesn't require much effort; if you look down long enough you're liable to see a bunch of them. That's life. It's more problematic when they actually come onto the platforms; and it's downright traumatic to be trapped in a moving train car with a panicking rat.

Anyway, I bring it up because it should give you a clear idea of the magnitude of New York City's vermin infestation. That specific 4:1 stat looked at rats, but their smaller cousins are certainly plentiful, too. Show me an older building in Manhattan that doesn't have rodents, particularly if it's in close proximity to the subway system and has a basement, and I will show you a unicorn. It's best to assume that every building in Manhattan has mice; it's best to pray that they don't have rats, too.

The theaters did their very best to keep the mice and rats away, but since they were surrounded by subway tunnels and so many other old buildings with subterranean levels, it might have been a futile endeavor. Even if they got rid of every single mouse, new ones could always find their way in. Theaters are warm spaces with many places to hide and many things to eat; they're very attractive to both people and rodents.

One summer at *The Graduate*, the mice carried out a veritable reign of terror. One of the supporting actresses, Alicia Silverstone, was a vegan and an ardent animal rights supporter, and we heard that she had requested that the theater refrain from killing the mice. As a result, they came out to say hi fairly regularly. At the other end of the spectrum, the feral cat that lived outside the Belasco earned his keep by taking care of much of the rodent population. The Belasco Kitty was deadly efficient and his presence was greatly appreciated; steps were taken to ensure that he was fed and had a warm place to sleep. He was, however, a messy hunter. The porters were sometimes faced with the horrifying task of cleaning up the decapitated rats that Kitty deposited in the stage door alley.

When I reported to my aisle at work, I would sometimes discover that mice had nibbled the stacks of Playbills during the night. At first I didn't realize what I was seeing; I thought perhaps the bundles had been dropped or caught in a door. After a while I learned to carefully inspect the Playbills before I even started preparing them for the walk-in, and to immediately throw away anything that had been partially eaten. Fortunately, the mice usually only got to the top few Playbills, and the rest were unscathed, but occasionally I had to discard entire bundles. For the money people paid to come to Broadway, I wasn't about to hand them mouse-chewed programs.

More troublesome were the mice that appeared during performances. They were afraid of neither noise nor crowds, so they'd strut right down the aisles. Usually, however, they were savvy enough to stay out of danger; they simply scampered along, freaked a few people out, and vanished before they got into trouble. I'm convinced it was a game for them.

The baby mouse at *The Phantom of the Opera* wasn't so lucky.

It was adorable, and it was sitting at the back of the orchestra in the middle of the aisle, curiously sniffing around. I spotted it at the exact moment that the house lights came up for intermission and the audience started spilling out of the seats. I rushed toward it, hoping to shoo it back into the safety of the vents.

"Don't. . . " The word left my mouth a second too late, and I was horrified to see a teenage girl in flip-flops stomp on the mouse. She apparently didn't realize, or care, that she'd stepped on a living creature, and she kept walking without breaking her stride or her conversation. I really, really don't want to believe that it was intentional, but to this day I have to wonder how the body of a small animal was imperceptible to someone in thin flip-flops.

I fought through the crowd to get to the mouse. It was still alive, but it was mutilated, broken, and apparently in an extreme amount of pain. A cluster of patrons gathered and watched as it writhed in agony on the carpet. All I could do was make a tent out of a Playbill and place it over the baby mouse, ask everyone to disperse, and call the porter.

The porter arrived almost immediately, scooped the poor mouse onto a shovel, and took it outside. He was a kindly, compassionate man, and I knew that he would humanely, or at least very quickly, put the mouse out of its considerable pain and misery.

For the rest of the evening, though, all I saw was its tiny, shattered body. For the rest of the night I was chilled by the knowledge that there was a teenage girl in the audience who had stepped on a living creature, left it in agony, and kept walking.

The Lullaby of Broadway

When you work in a theater, your schedule isn't exactly a traditional nine-to-five deal. You're working weekends, evenings, and holidays. You have only one day off every week. You might have long periods of unemployment when your theater is closed, during which time you might have to re-accustom yourself to a daytime schedule.

Broadway ushers are required to report to the theater an hour before curtain. Since most shows went up at eight o'clock for evening performances, I didn't have to be there until seven. For Wednesday matinees, my call time was usually one in the afternoon. Every now and then there would be variations on this theme: Sunday matinees; earlier curtain times on Tuesday nights.

When I lived in the Bronx I usually didn't make it home until midnight; when I lived in Manhattan, my commute was understandably much shorter. How do show folks commute, anyway? If they are typical New Yorkers, they might not know how to drive. If they're transplants or grew up in one of the outer boros and they do have a license, they're probably still not going to be driving to and from work. What with the expensive and elusive parking, the tolls and the traffic, bringing a car into Manhattan can be extremely unwise. As a result, a majority of theatrical employees opt to take mass transit, use a bicycle, or walk.

Public transit service can be infrequent in the evenings, though, depending on where one is going. Since most shows let out at ten or eleven at night it can be a problem, and theater folks sometimes end up dealing with long waits for the next bus or train.

This is especially true with the commuter lines that go to the outer boros, Long Island and New Jersey. Not everything runs around the clock like the subway system, either, and some neighborhoods are totally cut off from mass transit late at night. The last bus or train of the evening might be dangerously close to the time the curtain drops at end of the show. If you're ever waiting for an autograph at the stage door and an actor runs past you without stopping, don't assume he's a jerk. He might just be trying to ensure he's on that last pumpkin coach home.

Show people aren't the only ones who work night schedules, of course; New York City is full of people on evening and graveyard shifts. If you walk around Penn Station at three in the morning (I'm not actually suggesting you do this; we're talking hypotheticals) you will find scores of weary workers.

For me, there were some distinct advantages to working evenings. Night schedules are compatible with my natural circadian rhythm, because I'm a type B person. I always have been; I wager that I always will be. I do my best work in the dead of night; I'm barely functional in the morning. This isn't dependent on the amount of rest I get, either. I can get eight, ten or twelve hours of sleep; if I have to be at work at seven in the morning I'm still going to be a zombie. My personality actually changes once we hit midday. When I was in school my worst grades were typically in my first class of the day; the As appeared in my afternoon and evening courses.

Since I was home during the day, I got a lot done. Most people have to take off from work to go to doctor's appointments or bring their cats to the vet. I didn't. I had all the time in the world to run my errands in relative peace. I could hit the supermarket at eleven in the morning on Tuesdays and beat the after-work rush. I was always home when UPS deliveries arrived. I could go to school or find other work or volunteer opportunities during the day.

When I lived in the Bronx and took an express bus to the theater there was another lovely perk: I went against rush hour traffic. There were perhaps twenty people on board the bus with me. I'd occasionally see buses heading in the opposite direction as I looked out the window; they were invariably standing room only down to the front doors.

Since Broadway people work later into the night they also tend to sleep later in the morning unless they have a second job. When I was in college I got up at six because I had early morning classes, but I was always in such a state of fatigue that I frequently nodded off at school. Later, I was able to sleep until nine. That might sound lazy to anyone who is accustomed to already being at work at that hour, but it just gave me the eight hours of recommended rest.

It can be exceptionally hard for night shift workers to relate to those on traditional schedules. They tend to think you're lazy when you tell them that you sleep later, for instance. What they forget is that evening workers are just starting out when the nine-to-five sorts are finishing up for the day.

I recall an incident when I was trying to get a doctor's appointment at a local community clinic. I was in the throes of one of my respiratory infections, I was coughing up phlegm and I was so exhausted that I could barely stand upright. The center did take walk-in patients, but you had to be there at eight in the morning, when the doors opened, to get a spot. The line for walk-ins started at six. Since the clinic was a low-income facility that worked on a sliding scale, and it also happened to be clean, bright and well staffed, it was very popular with uninsured and underinsured people on the West Side.

I tried to explain to the nurse on duty that I was ill and needed to see a doctor. When the walk-in system was mentioned, I told her that it was almost impossible to get there so early in the morning since I worked nights. She sized me up, shook her head, and told me in a patronizing voice, "Well, just try to get up earlier, okay?" It was clear that she didn't get it, and that she thought I was just a lazy ass who didn't want to get out of bed in the morning.

The other negative to night and weekend work, and it is a large one, is that you have to take time off if you ever have any desire to engage in activities that other adults enjoy. Concerts? Parades? Workshops? Fuggedaboutit. And friends? Good luck. If you have friends who work on traditional nine-to-five schedules, you can forget about seeing them. They're working when you're home; you're home when they're working. On the holidays when they have time off you'll be doing extra performances. It takes effort to maintain friendships in such circumstances.

However, it is entirely doable. I'm a firm believer that we make the time to see those who are important to us, regardless of what else is going on. For years my interactions with my best friend were largely sandwiched between shows on Saturdays. She worked a conventional schedule so we couldn't see each other during the week. When I was over at *Phantom* I had Sundays off, but she went to church activities all day long. However, she loved Broadway, so she frequently came into the city on Saturdays to see shows. If I had an early shift at the Saturday matinee we'd meet up, spend four hours hanging out together, and then head back to the Theater District. We became masters at finding fun things to do in the city that did not take us too far from Broadway. We even saw the sights like tourists; there were trips to MoMA, the Pierpont Morgan Library, Rockefeller Center and the Empire State Building. In the evening she'd go to her Broadway theater to see the show she'd chosen; I'd go to mine, to work.

This tactic worked out well with other people, too; we met for lunch between shows on matinee days. I had a handful of friends who were night owls like me; they sometimes met me at the theater at ten or eleven and we took off to enjoy nocturnal New York together.

During my last five years at *Phantom*, I started calling out for performances so I could see my friends more often. We were allowed to take off two shows a week, and I decided to take advantage of that flexibility. When I was rocking out at an Aerosmith concert, gazing at Van Gogh's *Starry Night* at MoMA or feeling the ocean breeze as I watched a Cyclones baseball game with friends, I always thanked the stars for the opportunities I had.

Regardless, when one is marooned on a Broadway island, one inevitably begins to forge friendships at the theater. Proximity matters. Working closely, spending every weekend and holiday together and attending cast parties tend to be bonding exercises. The only problem is that the confidence is, in many cases, misguided. There are all sorts of caveats in business magazines about not confiding in your colleagues; those are unwisely ignored in Broadway theaters. Everyone tends to forget that by and large, any closeness might be as fake as the scenery flats on the stage. Nothing's real, and once you walk through the door in the set you'll find yourself staring at the bare brick wall at the back of the stage.

You hang onto your delusions, though. Sometimes it works out and you do find genuine friends. Other times you end up with pizza buddies with whom you can chat between shows. All too often, however, any relationships formed, and any personal information shared with colleagues, will become convoluted and may be used against you later.

Why? Broadway people love gossip. The he saids, she saids and they dids are of paramount importance. You spend two hours discussing a mishap at another theater because there's simply nothing else to talk about that everyone can agree on. And once you fall into this quagmire of gossip, it's hard to extricate yourself again.

When you're having an early dinner between shows at the little diner on 9th Avenue, you need to watch what you say; everyone around you is probably connected to Broadway in some fashion. Walking down 43rd Street, stopping at the supermarket at eleven at night or coming up out of the subway at Times Square, you're liable to run into someone you know. Hell's Kitchen is like Mayberry, when it comes down to it. A very catty, flashy version of Mayberry, but a small town nonetheless.

Sunday morning bagel feast with Greg and stage manager friends, backstage at Jackie Mason: Prune Danish *at the Royale.*

And as in all small towns, the gossip flies. It soars. It travels around underground networks, and if something of note happens in one theater, everyone else will know about it the same week. More likely, the same day.

I discovered just how potent this network was when I became a regular at the Majestic Theatre, home to *The Phantom of the Opera*. It really wasn't a surprise; I'd been a steady sub there for almost a year and everyone believed I would get the next open spot. When I did, it was without much ceremony; the chief turned to me, said, "You're in," and went back to her work. Nothing changed; I had the same locker as always and was assigned to the same aisle. It was a relief financially, since it meant that I didn't have to worry about work from week to week. *Phantom* wasn't showing any signs of closing any time soon, so uninterrupted employment on Broadway was probably guaranteed for another ten years, if I wanted to stick around that long.

A few days later I was in the elevator at the Equity building when another usher stepped in. We exchanged pleasantries, but for some reason, the atmosphere was tense. As we arrived on his floor he suddenly turned to me. "I heard you got transferred. You always do land on your feet." He exited the elevator without another word. I was stunned. I'd thought I was on good terms with this usher, and we'd gone out to dinner together a number of times, but he was genuinely angry that I was at the Majestic. I didn't even need to ask how he'd found out; I knew that the Broadway grapevine had worked its horrible magic.

I ambled down 44th toward the Belasco Theatre. The doorman was standing outside, and he smiled at me. "Congratulations on the Majestic!" This one left me dumbfounded. The Belasco was dark and between productions; there weren't even any ushers working there at the moment. Who was talking about me, and why? And was there really so little happening on Broadway that I was an interesting topic of conversation?

I later discovered that at least two ushers at other houses were angry that I'd been made a permanent staff member at the Majestic. They were bitching to their friends, and the word was getting around. And the more I heard, the more I decided that the gossip-mongers were downright pathetic.

Oscar Wilde once said, "There is only one thing in life worse than being TALKED ABOUT, and that is NOT being TALKED ABOUT." I get where he's coming from. On the other hand, I'd posit that being talked about in a negative fashion is worse than both of Oscar's choices.

The Ghost Light

The most magical time in a theater for me is when nobody's there. When it's dark and silent and the ghost light casts shadows on the walls of the auditorium, it's indescribably beautiful. It's the sort of enchantment that can never be replicated with pyrotechnics or clever stage effects; you could put the top actors of every era together and they'd never be able to come close to touching it.

When you walk through a darkened theater, you're immediately aware that it's brimming with energy. All the emotion felt by the actors and patrons stay within those walls. If it's just you and the ghost light, you feel it acutely, and it's enough to send those proverbial chills down your spine. The glow from that solitary lamp changes the entire appearance of the theater, and the bas-relief angels carved into the proscenium seem animated and alive. And perhaps they are.

Between shows the silent auditorium can also be a refuge for actors and crew members. As you pass through the rows of seats, you often spy dark shapes slumped here and there. They're not ghosts; they're show folks who are trying to rest up for the next performance.

Why are they there? On two-performance days – those are Wednesdays and Saturdays at most productions; perhaps also Sundays at shows geared toward family audiences – the split shift is a conundrum for many. After the matinee performance ends, the cast and crew usually don't have to work for another two or three hours, depending on their department. For ushers that have the early shift there's even more time; there are a good four or five hours of freedom.

Some show folks who live in Hell's Kitchen or somewhere else on the West Side are fortunate enough to be able to go home between performances. That's not the case for most, however. Most people don't live close enough. When I lived up in the Bronx, for instance, I had to leave two hours for the express bus to get to the Theater District. There would have been no way for me to go home on long matinee days. On short days, assuming I caught a bus at three, I'd get home around five. . . and then immediately need to get back on the bus to go back to work for the evening performance. It was a waste. When I lived in Manhattan I was able to get home on short shift days, but it still wasn't feasible on long afternoons, when I was getting out at 4:30 most of the time.

As many theater folks, I was stuck in midtown between shows, and I became adept at finding things to do. When I was a sub, I used my free time on Wednesdays to make my rounds to other theaters to pick up my checks from the previous week of work. Sometimes I'd been assigned to five or six different theaters over the course of the week, so I had many stops to make. I did my banking between shows, too.

On short matinee days, when I had about five hours to kill, I was often more ambitious. Sometimes I visited museums and other attractions. I wandered over to the main library branch on 42nd, where they had rotating free exhibits on the first floor. I tried to do as many errands as possible, scheduled eye appointments and picked up prescriptions. The city became my playground, and I wandered around taking photos.

Often, though, just I did what many other show folks did: I went out, I got my lunch, I took it back to the theater to eat, and I slept. If I happened to be working in a house that made a microwave available to the ushers, I'd bring some soup to nuke.

If you walk into a theater between shows on matinee days, you need to be quiet, because it's naptime. Some folks are lucky enough to have their own private dressing rooms or offices to sleep in. The rest of the actors, ushers and crew crash wherever they can find a quiet, comfortable place: the couches in the lounges; the seats in the auditorium; the carpeted floors; under the stage.

My favorite place to nap was the auditorium itself. I'd select a seat, close my eyes and rest under the kindly glow of the ghost light. As I leaned back in my seat I heard sounds around me, faintly, in the distance. A flurry of woodwind notes might drift in from the lobby as the house manager practiced his clarinet in his office. A new actor might be running through his songs with the musical director in the orchestra pit. One might pick up the echo of crew members calling to their friends from the stage door alley on the other side of the orchestra fire exits. The noise was comforting in the calm cocoon of the darkened theater.

At *Phantom* my wakeup call was the "Magical Lasso," or the Phantom's red killer noose. It would descend to the bare stage in all its ghastly glory, swinging and spinning slightly, so the crew could lock it in place for the next performance. The noose was always one of the first things the crew attended to during the pre-set. It meant that the lights in the auditorium would shortly be turned on, and that all of the nappers would groggily start to wake up. It was time to get back to work.

Accessible Prejudice

Over the last twenty years Broadway theaters have become increasingly accessible to disabled patrons. This is unquestionably a wonderful thing. In the 1990s and early 2000s the Shuberts and other theater owners worked architectural magic to make their venues welcoming to as many patrons as possible. Considering that many of the theaters they were dealing with were very old and were constructed in eras when the disabled were extremely marginalized, this was no small feat.

Accommodations for disabled patrons vary from theater to theater. There is almost always an accessible restroom somewhere on the first floor. These facilities were added to the older theaters one at a time, and were sometimes carved out of box office or coat check space. There are seats with retractable armrests for easy transfer from wheelchairs, for people with casts or braces, or for patrons of size. Some seats can be removed altogether, in only a few minutes, to accommodate patrons who need to remain in their wheelchairs.

Many of the pay phones are equipped with keyboards for text relay service for the hearing impaired. Sometimes the Theatre Development Fund also organizes special performances for deaf patrons, which involve rigging up a zipper board on the side of the stage that displays all the dialogue and lyrics. When I was working I always looked forward to these performances, since many of them also included live actors who interpreted the show in sign language. They stood in front of the stage on one side of the orchestra during the performance and signed to the hearing impaired patrons in front of them. These ASL interpretations were exquisitely beautiful, and I always found myself ignoring the performers who were singing and watching the ones who were signing. Every theater also has infrared assisted listening devices for the hearing impaired, which are free upon presentation of a credit card or ID.

There were some things I couldn't do for disabled patrons. I was not allowed to physically assist them in transferring from their wheelchair to a seat, for instance. If someone asked me to take their arm and lead them up the aisle or down the stairs, I couldn't do it. I could only walk in front of them to give them confidence and tell them how many steps they had left. That was for everyone's safety. I also couldn't obtain or return someone's assisted listening device; they had to do that themselves.

The other thing I couldn't do was to shield disabled guests from jerks who happened to be sharing space with them. And actually, this wasn't always restricted to patrons; on rare occasions I ran across intolerant staff members. I don't think I will ever forget the night at a certain show where the playwright, who was standing in the back of the orchestra, flatly refused to move out of our way so we could lead a blind woman to her seat.

One evening I was subbing at the Booth. It was a small, wood-paneled jewel box of a theater with a deceptively large façade and a lush downstairs lobby. It usually hosted serious plays with small casts, and as a result, the audiences tended to be older and more austere. Unfortunately, that didn't guarantee that they had any manners, much less compassion for others.

A physically disabled woman had come in. She'd been able to transfer from her wheelchair to a regular seat in the back of the orchestra. A few minutes after she was settled, I was called to the other end of her row by a group of elderly women.

"This is the *handicapped* section?!"
"We don't want to sit here."
"We don't want to sit with the wheelchair."
"What if we need to get up? How will we get past her?"
"Can't you move us?"

To use an old phrase to go with the old Booth Theatre, I was vexed. I silently reminded myself that if I didn't want to get fired, suspended or reprimanded, I couldn't say what was on my mind. Instead, I smiled pleasantly, told the women that I couldn't move them, and went back to ushering.

They didn't give up. Toward curtain time, one of them stood up and leaned over the railing to talk to me. She was only two feet away from the disabled patron.

"Can't you move us? This is the *handicapped* section." She lowered her voice. "I'll give you a tip." I glanced down. The disabled woman had clearly heard this exchange, and she was gazing at the carpet, frowning.

"I'm sorry but I can't move you, as I said before," I replied. I was again struggling mightily to bite my tongue. "If you want to move, you can talk to the house manager." She did; the response was a predictable no.

I turned to the disabled woman, who was still staring at the carpet. She'd come out for a nice night of theater, and she hadn't even made it to curtain time without being insulted. I hated that. I wished that I could move *her* so she wouldn't have to spend two hours stuck near such miserable people. All I could do was apologize and wish her a pleasant show. I knew that it wasn't enough, and that it wouldn't even begin to undo the damage that had been wrought by the obnoxious women. She wasn't going to remember the performance; she was going to remember that she had once again been ostracized and treated poorly by those around her.

Sometimes I really wished that I had all the powers that audience members thought I had. And in hindsight, even with my job on the line, I wish I'd told those women off.

Uncle Rigby

There are Broadway ushers everyone knows. Some are notorious for very negative reasons, but whether they have a good or bad rep, every face lights up with recognition when they check in with the head usher or someone mentions their names. They've been around the block for so many years that it's impossible not to have worked with them.

There was a sweet-natured usher who sang when he ran into people he knew. You usually heard him trilling away long before you spotted him. There was an extremely old woman who seemed to be completely dotty at first glance. When you spoke to her you learned that she had graduated from an Ivy League school. She had hip problems that made her walk slowly, but she was committed to swimming every day. There was an usher who unfortunately had hygiene problems and smelled bad. There was a Chinese woman who had gone through the Cultural Revolution and had stories to share about it; there were other intriguing faces that popped up again and again.

Rigby was one of these local celebrities.

I ran into him early on in my ushering career; he remained a constant presence until the mid-2000s. He had a steady house that happened to be closed on a regular basis, so he floated around as a sub most of the time.

He frequently referred to himself as Uncle Rigby, which made sense. He really *was* like a mad, short-tempered, eccentric uncle. He was short and squat and always had wild beard stubble; his glasses looked as though they hadn't been replaced since the early 1980s. His wardrobe when he was not in his ushering uniform consisted of Broadway t-shirts. He bought a new one from every show he saw and wore them in rotation. Rigby's other trademark was the pair of large plastic bags he always carried. I never did find out what they contained, but they bulged to the brim.

Rigby was a card-carrying member of Equity – properly Actors' Equity Association, the theatrical performers' union— but one never could pin down exactly where he'd performed. He claimed to have understudied on Broadway, but curiously, he could never be found in the Playbill, *Theatre World* or the Internet Broadway Database, either under his given stage name or his legal one.

Rigby also claimed to have slept with some Hollywood and Broadway luminaries and said that he'd been a singer for the USO. In addition, he told me that he had performed in a children's theater production of *Pinocchio*, that story about the little wooden boy who tells lies. I believed the last of these claims, and found the choice of show to be somewhat ironic.

Rigby and I occasionally had coffee before matinees. I was never sure if I actually wanted to go to these meetings or if I just felt guilty about saying no to Rigby. He frequently asked me personal questions; I always steered the conversation back to something safer. Rigby was a terrible gossip, and when he smiled and said, "You can trust me," I almost wanted to laugh in his face. He also had a biting wit, and sometimes served up insults slathered in pretty words. I couldn't decide if I enjoyed his company or if I found it a chore; the fact that I even had to debate it probably said it all.

Even if he told a lot of falsehoods and was snappy and acerbic, Rigby was a generous soul. He frequently received free tickets to shows and he always invited someone along. Before I grew to hate going to the theater, and when we were still friendly with each other, I was frequently his guest. We saw Encores! at City Center and obscure shows off-Broadway; fascinating productions I'd never have sought out on my own.

On numerous occasions he showed concern for others, too. Once, when I was fighting through yet another bout of illness, he stopped me and peered into my face. "You look ghostly," he said. "But not Alice Ghostley." There was no way to avoid laughing at that.

As time went on, I distanced myself from Rigby. I was tired of his veiled insults and gossiping, and I realized that I really didn't enjoy being around him at all. When I moved and got a new phone number, I chose not to give it to him. I still saw him around, and I still wished him well, but I turned down his social invitations.

And then one day I heard that he had died of a heart attack.

He was in his fifties, he was a Broadway usher, and he lived in a single-room occupancy hotel. He had called someone to tell them that he couldn't breathe and they'd sent an ambulance, but by the time he got to the hospital he was dead.

There was no funeral; there was no huge outpouring of support. There were very few tears shed for him. His death was a delicious bit of Broadway gossip, no more, no less. Most of the people he had invited to shows or treated to lunch seemed to be indifferent to his passing.

Rigby didn't have any family in New York, and his corpse remained in the morgue for quite some time. Finally, one of his relatives was located, and his cremated remains were transported to the Midwest. I was halfway sorry for Rigby that his ashes ended up there. He'd always expressed a great deal of contempt for the Midwest, and I'd ascertained that growing up in the region hadn't been entirely pleasant for him. On the other hand, I was extremely relieved that a family member had appeared. If Rigby's body had remained unclaimed, it probably would have ended up in Potter's Field.

Someone from the Actors Fund organized a small memorial for him. Fifteen people or so showed up; we sat around a long table in the conference room and told anecdotes about Rigby's life.

Nobody mentioned his Broadway claims. We all knew they had probably been lies.

At the end of the memorial, the moderator from the Actors Fund said, "I wish we'd had a chance to hear Rigby sing." I agree. I wish we had. I wish he'd actually had the Broadway credits he claimed, and most of all, I wish he'd had the chance to be more than Eleanor Rigby.

Broadway Kaleidoscope

Working in the Theater District and Times Square in the late 1990s and early 2000s was akin to being inside a kaleidoscope: all the colorful tiles around me were constantly being shuffled and reconfigured into new and exciting patterns. As soon as I became accustomed to them, someone shook the can again and everything tumbled into another position. Times Square and the Theater District have always been in flux, but during my tenure as an usher, the changes seemed to be happening at a lightning-quick pace.

When I first started working off-Broadway 42nd Street was a ghost town. The storefronts were closed and concealed behind brightly painted gates, and the New Victory was the only venue on the entire block that was open on a regular basis. There were many other historic theaters up and down the street, but they were, for the most part, disused.

The empty theaters on 42nd Street intrigued me. There was one in particular, with large iron mask medallions on the front doors and a ticket window, which aroused my curiosity. The signs on the doors identified it as the Pandora, an eerily apt name for an enigmatic space. Whenever I could, I tried to walk on the same side of the street as the Pandora so I could peer between the bars on the iron grates.

While there was no action at the Pandora, small changes did occasionally occur with other theaters up and down the street. For a while, inexplicably, snippets of poetry were posted on the abandoned marquees. The Liberty and Selwyn temporarily housed Fiona Shaw and Willem Dafoe, respectively, for solo shows. Shaw performed T.S. Eliot's *The Waste Land*, and the title couldn't have been more appropriate for the spectral street or the ramshackle Liberty Theatre. I found out about both productions too late to get tickets, unfortunately. In fact, when I saw the title of Dafoe's show *The Hairy Ape* on the Selwyn marquee, I think I may have mistaken it for more poetry.

At one point the Selwyn was also used as a Visitors' Center. I wandered in because I was excited about seeing the theater, and was disappointed when I found that the Center didn't extend to the auditorium. Until the mid-nineties, the Apollo Theatre was the site of the Academy nightclub. I did get to see that, thanks to an opening night party for the New Victory Theater that was hosted there.

By the time I started working on Broadway 42nd Street was in the midst of its slow creep back to life. The Pandora, which was actually the Empire, which was originally the Eltinge after female impersonator Julian Eltinge, was actually picked up and hauled down to the end of the block. The façade, lobby, proscenium and various elements of the auditorium were restored for use as the entrance to the AMC cinema. I haven't a clue what happened to the door medallions, but larger versions of the masks are still visible on the ceiling of the AMC lobby. The architectural elements that identified it as the Pandora were actually movie props from the early 1990s and were not historic at all; the theater had been used as a location for an action film and they'd never cleared away the set dressings. The Liberty also survived, but spent most of the last two decades sealed off behind a wall. The poor Times Square Theatre has changed hands several times; nobody seems to know what to do with it.

The new Lyric Theatre incorporates the façade of the demolished 1903 Lyric Theatre and architectural elements from both the Lyric and Apollo. The New Amsterdam and Selwyn, along with the Biltmore and Studio 54 further uptown, have all returned to use as legit Broadway theaters. While I wasn't around in the seventies to experience its decadence, Studio 54 was still familiar to me as the former site of the Ritz nightclub from the early 1990s. I had gone to the Ritz when I was fourteen; it was mildly amusing to me that the site of my underage rock club kid exploits had gone legit.

However, some theaters still fell through the cracks. Between 1995 and 2010 I watched more than ten of them go down. Henry Miller's Theatre (named for the turn of the century playwright, not the *Tropic of Cancer* author), the Harris, the Apollo and the Lyric all died. There was no funeral for the Central, which was concealed behind the Lunt-Fontanne and Ho-Jo's and was quietly destroyed. On 42nd Street a number of movie houses were picked off: the Rialto, with its wavy blue terra cotta façade, was one of them. Some tiny theaters on 42nd Street between 7th and 6th also bit the dust; they were so small, and apparently so insignificant, that nary a word was said about their demise. The Ideal Theatre on 8th Avenue, which had long been a peep show, was also demolished.

Once 42nd Street came back to life, the businesses there seemed to appear and vanish at an alarmingly rapid clip. The Disney Store popped up adjacent to the lovingly restored New Amsterdam Theatre, but then popped away again as a string of slick retail outlets opened along the Deuce. An ancient Egyptian goddess spread her gilded wings over the entrance to the Museum Store for several years, but finally flew away. A behemoth Easy Internet cyber café with hundreds of computer terminals was resplendent in its 1970s orange décor, but it logged off before 2010. Warner Brothers opened a fantastic three-story extravaganza of a store that was decorated with murals parodying Broadway shows; it only lasted until 2001 or 2002. Ellen's Dine-O-Mat, a cute restaurant that was a tribute to 1940s automats, opened at the corner of 43rd and 7th; it went out of business after only a few years when the building that housed it was demolished.

The proscenium and ceiling mask medallion of the Eltinge Theatre, restored as the lobby of the AMC cinema.

Further uptown in the Theater District, many beloved haunts closed in the late 1990s and 2000s. Oh La La, the tiny coffee shop in the Marriott Marquis Hotel that sold the best hot chocolate ever produced in the Western Hemisphere, was replaced by a Starbucks. Teatro Pizza, where the slices topped with baked ziti provided a carbo-load that could pull even the weariest usher through matinee day, went out. Over by the Winter Garden, a fast food joint that included a Pizza Hut, a KFC and several other chains was closed. It had all the charm of a subway station, but it also had large Broadway posters on every wall. Speaking of subway stations, just downstairs from the Pizza Hut in the 50th Street 1/9 stop lurked Siberia, a tiny bar that had had reportedly served as a rendezvous point for Soviet KGB spies during the Cold War. That eventually went away, too.

A fair number of ushers and crew members have been kicking around Broadway for decades; they've developed preservationist hearts along the way. Many attended Save Our Theaters protests in the early 1980s, when five Broadway theaters, including the Morosco, the original Helen Hayes and the former Astor, were unceremoniously knocked down. Some were even present on the Morosco's final day, when protesters both famous and anonymous were carried away in police vans.

Thus, many ushers, including myself, tried to make one final pilgrimage to any restaurant that was closing around Midtown. I headed over to McHale's, Barrymore's and the Cheyenne Diner between shows to have one last late lunch. Even the Howard Johnson's on 46th, which we all typically avoided due to its rude wait staff and unimpressive food, was given a goodbye.

Somewhere along the way, I realized I didn't have photos of the theaters, shops and restaurants that were disappearing. To this day I deeply regret that I never spent a few hours walking up and down pre-gentrification 42nd Street, taking photos. It just never crossed my mind. I'd never even thought to take a photo of myself at work, either.

I started documenting as many things as I could around the Theater District, including my own employment when possible. When I was dealing with film, which was expensive to buy and develop, I had to be conservative with my projects. When I switched over to a digital camera I essentially could take an unlimited amount of photos, and I did.

Taking my cue from Berenice Abbott, I tried to document things that might neither be preserved nor noticed. I photographed street signs and old marquees; the shops in Times Square and public art, and the exteriors of the little theaters on 42nd St. before they were pulled down. I attended one of the final performances of *Urinetown* at Henry Miller's; I was not interested in seeing the show as much as I wanted to explore the theater before it was demolished. I couldn't get any photos in the auditorium, but when I was alone on a stairwell I whipped out my camera and snapped a few clandestine shots. Since the entire place was going to be gone in a matter of months and I wasn't taking photos of the set or the performance, I didn't feel particularly bad about it. I returned to Henry Miller's Theatre later on to capture the exterior on film.

I couldn't stop the changes that were sweeping through the Theater District, but I could certainly document them.

I remembered to photograph one of my favorite old theatrical landmarks in Times Square, the façade of the Show Folks' Shoe Shop.

New Year's Eve

One of my college professors once told me, "In the theater, holidays mean one thing: extra performances." He was correct. On Broadway, the show doesn't stop for Christmas, Thanksgiving, Labor Day, Passover, Arbor Day, Halloween or anything else. Extra performances are often tacked onto the schedule during holiday periods, particularly Christmastime, to capitalize on the huge tourist crowds visiting New York City. These shows are almost always sold out.

As an usher, I worked more holidays than I could ever count. The production team sometimes tried to give us a break, but there was always a tradeoff. If we didn't work Christmas Eve, we'd be there on Christmas. If we didn't work Thanksgiving, we'd have two shows on Black Friday. Taking time off during holiday weeks was frowned upon for obvious reasons, whether one was cast, crew or front of house staff.

Those who needed to travel out of town to see family found this very problematic; those of us with relatives nearby usually found ways to make it work. Luckily for me, I was in the latter group. My Mom lived in the city and I usually saw her on Christmas Eve. As such, I didn't mind working on Christmas night; by evening the celebration was over so it didn't matter if I went to work. If nothing else, since most people were home it was an easy commute for me.

I don't observe Thanksgiving at all, so working on that holiday never bothered me either. I learned early on never to mention this to patrons. When they asked "Did you enjoy

Thanksgiving?" and I cheerfully told them that I didn't celebrate it, they looked at me as though I were a space alien, a heathen, or both. I still remember the expression of shock and horror on one particular patron's face when I let him in on that secret. Getting into the wheres, whys and hows of my refusal to observe Thanksgiving would have made their heads spin, and it was neither the place nor the time for a discussion of that nature. I simply learned to smile, nod, thank them for their question and tell them that I'd had a good day. That wasn't lying; I usually *had* had a good day. I hadn't specified that I'd had a good *Thanksgiving*.

The only holidays I particularly cared about, other than Christmas, were Halloween, Mother's Day and my birthday. Halloween at the theater could be great fun, since some house managers allowed us to work in costume. Thus, in various years I greeted patrons on the aisle as a cat, a ballet dancer, Ginny Weasley from the Harry Potter series, and a gothic version of Pippi Longstocking. As time went on, though, I found that I preferred to call out for Halloween. I started volunteering as a puppeteer in the Village Halloween Parade. Carrying large puppets for several miles and making them dance and interact with the screaming crowds was far more physically taxing than ushering, but it was also infinitely more fun.

On my birthday I didn't want to be anywhere near the theater, or even New York: I generally used my two weeks of annual unpaid leave and got out of Dodge. And if I happened to be working at a production with Sunday performances, I called out on Mother's Day. Unfortunately, since Sunday shows were almost always matinees, there really wasn't a way to work *and* travel to an outer boro to see my mother. Mom was just more important.

The only holiday that made me groan was New Year's Eve. Sometimes the management made December 31 our dark day; perhaps they knew just how difficult it was for the cast and crew to get to and from work. In other years they scheduled the December 31 performances as matinees so everyone could get out of the Theater District before nightfall and avoid the worst of the chaos.

Every now and then, however, we were unlucky and had an evening performance on New Year's Eve.

What was so bad about New Year's Eve? Well, let's break it down. Most of the theaters are right off Times Square, a stone's throw from the site of the New Year's Eve ball drop. Folks camp out all day for a prime spot, and by the evening Times Square is crammed with hundreds of thousands of people. To facilitate security, the NYPD always blocks off the streets around Times Square. You can't blame them; they have to keep everyone safe and there's a finite limit to the number of people that Times Square can accommodate. However, if you're trying to get to work and your place of business is on one of the streets with limited access, it's a complete pain in the ass. In theory, the police are supposed to let you through the barricades if you have legitimate reason to be on a certain street. If you live there, you're staying at one of the hotels, you're working or you're seeing a Broadway show, you're supposed to show some proof to the police officers, and they're supposed to allow you through the barricades to continue to your destination. In practice, though, you might end up being redirected over and over again.

Broadway theater employees usually have an excellent rapport with the beat cops that patrol Times Square. On New Year's Eve, however, they're not around, and the new cops aren't necessarily familiar with those who work or live in the area. One year the police refused to let an entire group of ushers past the barricades. Someone finally managed to get in touch with one of the house managers; he had to go down to the barricade and personally vouch for his staff.

To combat this, the next year the Shuberts equipped us with photo ID cards and letters from our house managers. Even these had little effect, however. When I presented my documents at the barricades on 45th and 6th, I was unlucky enough to get the one police officer in Times Square that hated Broadway in every way, shape and form. How did I know this? When people stepped up to the checkpoint and showed him letters or ID cards from other employers, including those on the same street as my theater, he let them pass immediately. When someone with Broadway tickets or theatrical employee identification approached, he shunted them off to the side and told them to wait.

I watched for nearly ten minutes as numerous individuals from other businesses all over Times Square were allowed through the barricades; I watched as the cluster of Broadway people grew. Eventually I approached the cop again.

"Sir, I'm sorry, but I do have to get to work. . . " I tried.

"WAIT! I told you to wait! Just wait!" he screamed. Apparently, in addition to hating live theater, he had a very short fuse. I backed away and found another officer on the other side of the checkpoint. As soon as I showed him my credentials he opened the fence for me, let me through, and wished me a pleasant evening.

Walking through the restricted zone on New Year's Eve was like traveling through a post-apocalyptic city. There was nobody there, and that absolutely, positively never happens in New York City. Even early in the morning, when there aren't many pedestrians out, there are still cars. This time? Nada. I gulped as I walked down 45th toward 8th Avenue. The Lyceum Theatre in the middle of the block was dark for the night, the lucky bastards.

As I approached Broadway and 7th, Times Square proper, the roar of the crowd assailed me, and I was actually pushed backward by the force. Flashing lights. Horns. Noisemakers. Music blasting from speakers; vibrant colors glittering on the giant television screens and billboards. I walked down a narrow path; on either side of me, separated and controlled by metal fencing, there were thousands and thousands of people, all of whom were screaming.

At every street corner there was another battalion of cops. There was no way to speak to them over the din; I just flashed my ID and got waved along. By the time I reached the theater I was exhilarated from the sheer rush of energy I'd experienced.

I don't think I will ever have the desire to watch the ball

drop in Times Square. I don't even bother with it on television. If I ever had the chance to walk through those barricades again, though, I'd probably do it. Being on the outside of the throng, and watching it pulse around me, is how I'd always want to do New Year's Eve in New York.

Crystals on the Times Square Ball, on exhibit in the Times Square Visitors' Center.

Party Hearty

The Kat and the Kings *holiday party.*

If you want to discern the true character of a Broadway production there's really only one question you need to ask: were the ushers invited to the opening night party? The shows that extend invitations to the ushers, merchandising crew and bartenders are generally the better ones. Why? They treat the front of house folks as valued members of the team.

The large Cameron Mackintosh musicals, *Phantom, Cats and Les Mis*, are excellent about this, for what it's worth. Everyone I knew who worked at *Cats or Les Misérables* told me that they were invited to the closing parties for their shows. In the six years I worked as a regular at *Phantom*, the ushers were never excluded from a single celebration. In 2006, when *Phantom* broke *Cats'* record to become the longest running show on Broadway, we even received formal, personalized invitations to the black-tie party at the Waldorf Astoria Hotel along with all the other guests. I still have mine at home.

I went to some other smashing parties in my time at *Phantom*. The most memorable was on one of the top floors of the Dream Hotel, in a magical space with flickering candles and long corridors leading to secret rooms. On other occasions, when there wasn't a large outside party for one reason or another, the cast and crew all gathered onstage at the Majestic for cake and pizza. Clearing the theater on party nights could be a challenge; the audience would see that there was something fun that was about to happen and they'd try to stay (Nope. Sorry.).

The closing party for *Enchanted April* was held at a wonderful Italian restaurant down the block from the Belasco Theatre, where we all sat at long tables to laugh and eat together. Considering that the show was set mostly in Tuscany, ending the run with some good Italian food was most appropriate. John Leguizamo's *Sexaholix* gave everyone "backstage pass" laminates for the opening night bash at Ruby Foo's. *Def Poetry Jam* had a great closing party. Even though we were all sad that the production had met an untimely end, we genuinely enjoyed spending one last evening together.

The shows that exclude the ushers, merchandising staff and bartenders from the opening and closing night parties never inspire the same enthusiasm. When the front of house learns that they're not invited, the morale instantly plunges. It's not about going to a party and getting free food; it's not about getting into the chic restaurant or nightclub where the event is happening. It's about knowing the attitude of the production staff toward the employees. When the ushers are included, the message that is conveyed is, "We acknowledge that you work with us, we like you, and we don't think that you are invisible." When the front of house staff is

The cake at Phantom*'s 20th anniversary party.*

excluded, the production and management teams are making it crystal clear that they don't think that the ushers count. Their contributions don't matter. They're just plebeians.

While I would never purport that ushers have anywhere near the same influence on the production as the actors, musicians, stage managers or stagehands, they really do their damndest to ensure that everything out front goes smoothly. That, in turn, means that the actors, musicians, stagehands and stage managers might have an easier time doing their jobs.

At *Kat and the Kings*, a musical from Cape Town, South Africa that played at the Cort Theatre in 1999, there was a definitive disconnect between the wishes of the management office, the house staff and the actors. Several of the younger ushers struck up friendships with members of the cast, most of whom were excited to be in New York. These acquaintanceships and friendships were genuine, and some of us kept in touch even after the show closed. At Christmas the entire theater came together for a party and a huge Secret Santa. If we were sitting in the audience during the show the performers always acknowledged us when they could; I always looked for my Act I wink from Luqmaan Adams. Staff at the management office and one of the producers, the wonderful Willette Klausner, also became friendly with us. We had a common goal: we were all trying to help this striking little show find its wings and fly.

This was at odds with the philosophy of the company manager, unfortunately. He was a rather nebbish, stoic fellow, and he never said two words to the ushers, unless it was to offer criticism or express his annoyance or contempt toward us. It was clear that he considered the ushers to be completely repulsive.

Kat and the Kings closed after only four months or so on Broadway. The ushers did not receive invitations to the closing night party. However, a friend in the cast, Alistair Izobell, invited me anyway. Since I'd been asked to attend by a cast member, I walked over to the restaurant with two friends, Gene and Bob. They had attended a lot of performances and they'd also been invited to the party.

Our very best buddy, the company manager, met us at the threshold. He ignored Gene and Bob and addressed me directly. "I'm sorry, but the ushers were not invited," he said. I stared at him for a second, hoping that he was joking, but he was dead serious.

"I'm here as a personal guest of Alistair," I retorted. "Not as an usher."

"Well, *Alistair*. . . "

"Stop it!" There was another shadow in the doorway, and Willette bustled over to us, cutting off the manager mid-sentence. "They're invited. She's been a great supporter of the show." She turned to me. "Please come in." Bob, Gene and I awkwardly walked into the room.

"Thank you," I said. I didn't even hear the response; Willette had moved off to speak privately with the management troll. She was on my side, and I was grateful.

With Luqmaan Adams at Kat and the Kings.

Alistair popped over to see what had happened, and someone else handed me a plate of pasta. As I tucked into my ziti I looked around the room. What I saw reinforced just how much this particular manager hated the ushers. The merchandising people had been invited, and I spotted at least one of the theater bartenders at the back of the dark room. There were also several superfans. I could have been wrong, but I wagered that none of them had been stopped at the door. If Gene and Bob had showed up without me, they probably would have been admitted without a fuss too. This guy had actively excluded the ushers while inviting just about everyone else in the entire theater, both front and back of house. I didn't know what we'd ever done to him, but the grudge was apparently much deeper than I had originally thought.

For the rest of the night I caught the management troll glaring at me off and on, especially when I was chatting with friends from the show. It was kind of sad to think that he had so much hostility invested in someone who really hadn't wronged him. When I spotted him talking to the house manager, I knew I needed to do something. I didn't care if he hated me, but I couldn't have him potentially jeopardizing my future employment.

The house manager stood to one side of the room, nursing a drink. He raised his eyebrows when I approached him.

"Listen, I want you to know that I didn't crash this party. I really *was* invited by someone in the show, and I didn't think it would be an issue." He needed to know that.

He regarded me quietly. "Yes, I know. And I think you all should have been invited, anyway." Relief flooded through me. With one notable exception, I was among friends.

Broadway Bloopers

Do the actors ever screw up? Of course they do. When it happens, it's often conversation fodder for everyone. It's not about Schadenfreude as much as it's about variety. When you've seen the same show hundreds of times you tend to become desperate for some deviation from the standard performance. Bloopers are entertainment for all, as long as no one gets hurt or fired.

At *Phantom* there were several instances where the actor playing Joseph Buquet didn't make it onstage in time for his big number, "Magical Lasso." If you haven't seen the show, it's a scene where a grizzled old stagehand, Buquet, scares the young ballerinas of the Opera Populaire by regaling them with horror stories of the "opera ghost" who lives under the theater. When Madame Giry, the ballet mistress, shows up, the girls scurry away. Giry is left onstage with Buquet; she essentially tells him, "Shut up and stop talking about the Phantom or you're going to be murdered in a horrible fashion, just so you know." Much more poetically, of course.

The first time I saw this happen, the dancers just looked uncertainly at each other until Meg, the most visible ballerina and supporting character, got up and tried to tell a ghost story. The second time, Meg popped right up and recited all of Buquet's lines perfectly. In both cases, Giry had to direct her lines to Meg instead of Buquet. It actually fits plausibly into the story: Giry spends a good portion of Act I reprimanding the ballerinas as it is, and Meg is her daughter.

There were so many special effects and props in *Phantom* that it was inevitable that some of them would fail occasionally. The drapes that cover the golden angel and gilded proscenium are pulled away by stagehands dressed in period costumes during the overture at the top of the show. They step into the boxes closest to the stage, yank down the drapes, and step out again. The fabric is rigged to fall away effortlessly if it is tugged the right way, but every now and then I saw it get stuck. Instead of making his pull and disappearing, the poor stagehand would end up standing there, hauling on the drapes. They always gave way eventually, fortunately.

In the climatic final scene of the show the Phantom ensnares Raoul in the "magical lasso," a garish red noose that seems to float in the air. I witnessed a few performances where the noose didn't work properly, so the Phantom just used the Force instead and gestured toward Raoul with deliberate hand movements. Raoul got with the program instantly, obligingly froze in place, and writhed in pain.

At the very end of the show, the Phantom sits down on his elaborate throne and throws a cape over his head. As Meg and several other characters climb down a metal gate to invade his lair, he vanishes. When Meg reaches the throne, she rips away the cape. The Phantom is gone, but he's left his mask on the seat of the chair.

Sometimes the Phantom's chair doesn't work and he can't go anywhere. Meg is quickly given a heads up so she doesn't tear the cape away. Instead, she just grabs the mask, if possible; or kneels quietly by the throne. I never saw this myself, but I was told that on at least one occasion when the chair didn't work, Meg didn't hear the warning and ripped the cape away anyway. She discovered the Phantom slumped over on his throne, apparently dead.

At *Les Misérables* there were chair malfunctions too. In one scene early in the show, there's a confrontation between Inspector Javert and Jean Valjean in a hospital room. Valjean is at the hospital to visit the dying Fantine and reassure her that he will care for her daughter, Cosette. Just after Fantine expires, Javert shows up and attempts to arrest Valjean. The two men end up fighting at Fantine's bedside. They sing, they stalk each other, and eventually Valjean picks up a chair, smashes it to pieces, and brandishes a jagged bit of wood at Javert to hold him off.

There was one particular Valjean actor who just wasn't friends with the breakaway prop chair. The thing seemed to get the better of him on a regular basis. He'd pick it up and it wouldn't break. It broke before he had a chance to smash it. He tapped it lightly on the floor and the entire thing weakly crumbled. The actor playing Javert always pressed his lips together in a fierce scowl, but if you looked closely, you could see that he was trying to avoid laughing. He did his very best to make the audience believe he was very, very intimidated by the pitiful bits of wood that were scattered across the stage. A regular *Les Mis* usher told me that there was even a performance where the wood from the chair hit Fantine as she reposed on her deathbed, and the poor actress had to break character and raise her hands to protect her face. Apparently, malfunctioning prop chairs have the power to resurrect the dead.

Over at *Cats*, most of the errors I witnessed were small. The lights on the Siamese cat costumes in "Growltiger's Last Stand" didn't always illuminate; the wings on the beetle outfits in the Gumbie Cat tap dance didn't always open. Occasionally a performer slipped and fell. There were several flashpots on the stage; during the "Mr. Mistoffelees" number Mistoffelees pointed at them and they "magically" exploded with sparks and smoke. I was told that when the charges didn't go off it was sometimes a matter of safety; if the crew felt that one of the performers was too close to a flashpot they didn't discharge it.

In *The Life*, a dark musical about prostitutes in 1970/80s Times Square that played at the Ethel Barrymore Theatre, Pamela Issacs was supposed to storm offstage during one particularly tense scene. One evening when I was there the door in the set wouldn't open for her, so she couldn't make her exit. She struggled with it for a moment, and then regally stalked around the edge of the set to take her leave, her head held high.

In the musical version of *Jekyll & Hyde* at the Plymouth, the eponymous characters went through several dramatic transformations onstage. The metamorphoses were fueled by injections of Nasty and Nice serums Jekyll had created in his laboratory. During one performance, at a point in the show where Hyde was being especially creepy and scary, the syringe he was about to jam into his arm slipped out of his hand and rolled away. The actor had to crawl around the set to find it, since the scene couldn't continue without the injection sequence.

This wouldn't have been particularly noteworthy if not for the fact that the actor muttered, in his perfectly eerie Hyde voice: "Oops."

My Broadway Debut

Singing "Help Is on the Way" onstage at the New Amsterdam Theatre, 2006.
Photo with permission of Broadway Cares/Equity Fights AIDS.

In the spring of 2006, a few months after *The Phantom of the Opera* became the longest-running show in Broadway history, I made my official performing debut on the Great White Way. You can blame *Phantom* for that. The show had been invited to sing David Friedman's song, "Help Is on the Way" at the New Amsterdam Theatre as part of the grand finale of Broadway Cares/Equity Fights AIDS' spring benefit show, the Easter Bonnets. *Phantom* has long been a huge supporter of BC/EFA, and every fall and spring the show embarks on a massive fundraising drive.

Being asked to close the Bonnets was an incredible honor. The show brought together performers and crew from almost every play and musical on Broadway, as well as many off-Broadway and national tour productions. Every show put together a skit, a song or a dance and designed an Easter bonnet. Some productions took a silly approach; others were serious, and the range of talents on display was remarkable.

I was stunned when the stage managers at *Phantom* invited everyone to participate: ushers, bartenders, merchandising crew, stagehands, and wardrobe. *Phantom* was always wonderful to its support staff, but this really went above and beyond. They had just handed me a chance to sing on a Broadway stage.

I decided to participate; so did another usher, Stacy. When we arrived at the first rehearsal, things were awkward. The ballet dancer who handed out the sheet music passed us over even though we were standing right in front of her. I had to wave her over again once she'd walked away, and she made it clear that she was not thrilled that we had been included. I didn't care; she was not in charge, and we had been given a direct invitation. As I looked around the room I was relieved to see that many backstage and front of house folks were participating; I spotted a few of the bartenders, some merch staff, makeup artists and crew members.

There are two major reasons why I'm never going to be a singer. Both of them reared their disagreeable heads and complicated my Bonnets rehearsals. One, I can't read music. I suppose that's a biggie. Two, singing in harmony totally throws me off, since I can't really hear the others who are doing my part. My alto voice is pleasant and on-key, however, so I resolved to make it work. I stayed after rehearsal, asked the musical director, Jonathan, to play through my part for me, and made a recording so I could practice at home.

And practice I did. I didn't care that my voice was going to be swallowed up under the professionals' work; I didn't care that I couldn't sing even a fraction as well as they could. I still wanted to do my best. It was a Broadway show, it was for BC/EFA, and I was taking it very seriously. By the day of the first performance, I was ready to go.

I'd been to the New Amsterdam Theatre once before, but as an audience member, not a performer. As I walked through the lobby I remembered the protocol: every employee entering the theater to work, or leaving at the end of the night, needed to say hello or goodbye to Olive Thomas, the beautiful Ziegfeld Girl. Olive's ghost had been involved in numerous incidents around the theater, and some of the New Amsterdam ushers who subbed at *Phantom* had told me stories about their interactions with her. I didn't know if I counted as an employee but I didn't want to take chances; as I passed through the lobby doors I whispered a greeting to lovely Olive.

When I checked in I was presented with a performers' lanyard and laminate. We were all invited to autograph the production show posters, which would be sold later to benefit BC/EFA. As I took up the Sharpie and added my signature to each poster, I was reeling. Broadway debut, performer's laminate, autographs. Where did it end? By the time we were escorted backstage I was giddy.

Backstage, I almost lost my nerve when I bumped into one of the giant *Lion King* masks in the corridor and nearly toppled it over. In the back of my mind I halfway feared that someone was going to pop up, tell me I didn't belong there, and cart me away to the front of the house. Fortunately, it didn't happen. I was under the stage at the New Amsterdam Theatre, and I was about to make my Broadway debut.

We assembled onstage in the darkness. The entire *Phantom* orchestra accompanied us, and each of us singers carried a music stand and chair for one of the musicians. On the other side of the scrim, the 102-year-old Ziegfeld Girl, Doris Eaton Travis, did a vintage dance number. I could barely hear her words and I saw her only as a silhouette against the backdrop; but I savored every second of it. I'd read Eaton Travis's memoir, *The Days We Danced,* and I was awestruck to be less than six feet away from a woman who had performed in the *Ziegfeld Follies of 1918*. What did it mean to experience a century? What was it like for her to return to the stage on which she had danced almost a hundred years ago? I couldn't even imagine.

Usually before performances I try to center down. This time, I simply watched Doris Eaton Travis's shadow as it flickered across the scrim. When the number concluded, I clapped heartily. As I looked around, I realized that the entire *Phantom* ensemble was applauding along with me. We all knew we had been privileged to be in the presence of true greatness.

And then it was our turn. I set the chair and music stand down, got into position in the chorus, and sang. I'd become a tiny part of the New Amsterdam's history too.

In total, I got to sing on the New Amsterdam Theatre stage three times: once for the dress rehearsal; twice for the actual performances. It was enough. Being up there even once was more than I ever could have asked for.

"Thank you, Olive," I whispered as I left the New Amsterdam after the last performance. I meant it.

Act II: Shows and Theaters

New Victory Theater

The New Victory Theater – deliberately spelled with 'er,' and not the more flowery and common 're' – held its very first opening night party at the Apollo Theatre on 42nd Street. The Apollo, at that time, was home to the Academy rock nightclub, and was in its last stages of existence altogether. Within a few years, it would be demolished for the construction of the Ford Center for the Performing Arts, now known as the Lyric Theatre.

The caterers had set up large candlelit tables of food in the stark, lonely space. We piled delicacies onto plates and roamed through the empty theater, our voices echoing. Since there weren't any seats on the floor, many of us perched on the edge of the stage.

I didn't chat much with my colleagues; instead, I looked around. The Apollo was intriguing even in its decayed state. At one time it must have been a wonderful theater. There were fanciful cherubs sculpted into the proscenium arch; plaster ivy climbed the walls; and a beautiful dome dominated the ceiling. It was all rotting away. The seats in the orchestra had been removed and replaced by a wooden dance floor. The wings were still intact, but a red brick structure had been built on the stage. Peeling paint was everywhere. I was profoundly sad to see how neglected it all was.

At the end of the night, I left the theater via a decrepit unused passage and walked out onto a cold, dark 42nd Street. The only real illumination on the street came from the gleaming New Victory Theater; it sat in stark contrast to the abandoned buildings that lined the rest of the block.

The New Victory was the first of the disused 42nd Street theaters to be restored and returned to regular use. It had followed the same pattern as most of the other theaters on 42nd: it had started life in 1900 as a Broadway performance venue, had switched over to movies sometime in the 1940s, and had finally become an adult cinema. The building itself, and all of its elaborate architectural elements, had been left to deteriorate. Fortunately, the New 42nd Street Corporation came to the rescue in the early nineties and painstakingly renovated and restored the theater.

The New Victory and the story of its restoration intrigued me and fostered a love of theater architecture that has persisted to this day. I recorded documentaries and news footage about it on TV. When I didn't have anything else to do at the theater I walked around the balcony to study the putti on the ceiling dome. I wandered up and down 42nd Street on my breaks and looked at the other old venues.

I eventually bought a copy of Nicholas van Hoogstraten's *Lost Broadway Theatres* and studied every page. The book contained a very helpful map of the Theater District, and I noted where the extant venues were located and looked for signs of them when I passed by on the street. The New Victory was in van Hoogstraten's book, and I was thrilled to learn that David Belasco and Mary Pickford had both been associated with the theater. Belasco had owned and managed it for a while; Pickford had performed there as a young girl.

Just as Pickford had been expected to be wholesome and friendly as America's Sweetheart, the New Victory wanted its ushers to be personable, fresh-faced and cheerful. The customer was always right; we were always to smile and nod; and we were to leave the heavy lifting and patron conflict resolutions to the managers. The management held meetings to regroup after every performance and sent us to customer service and résumé-building workshops.

We were outfitted in casual black t-shirts or sweatshirts with the New Victory logo and were provided with large red shoulder bags to hold our programs. More than once, when I worked as a Broadway usher later on, I wished I still had one of those satchels to carry my Playbills. The New Vic's ushers performed various duties on a rotating schedule, from running the elevator to taking tickets; and after the performance ended and the patrons left we were expected to help with some basic pickup.

The New Victory has developed a very well-respected Usher Corps program that specifically employs, trains and mentors teenagers, but during the first season a much wider span of ages and backgrounds was represented. I was a teenager myself, but as far as I could see I was one of the younger people on staff. I'd found the job through my college, since one of the house managers had a connection to my school. He'd posted a "help wanted" flyer on my department's bulletin board; I'd responded. It was a good match: I was interested in working on Broadway and the New Victory was close enough to start. It was also compatible with my class schedule. Most of the performances were at night, and the matinees were easy to work around, more or less.

The New 42nd Street, which ran the New Victory, wanted to create a family venue with an appealing and diverse schedule of programming. In the first season they were successful. . . mostly. The Montreal-based human-only circus Cirque Éloize opened the theater with a fantastic production that included both aerial acts and comedy. I'd just started to learn French; several members of the troupe patiently helped me with my pronunciation and taught me some new vocabulary. Once or twice they even let me pick up their clubs and try my hand at juggling, even though it was painfully obvious that I wasn't particularly good at it.

The performers of Cirque Éloize posed onstage for a photo op for the ushers. Sadly, I didn't have a good camera yet.

Julie Taymor's *The Green Bird* ran for a very prosperous month, and both Taymor and composer Elliot Goldenthal were frequently seen around the theater. There were two versions of the show: a children's edition for matinees and an adult one for the evenings. Truth be told, there wasn't much of a difference, just a slight softening of some of the jokes and innuendos. In addition, the actress playing Pompeana, a living statue, was nude and covered in white body paint in the regular version of the show. For the matinees the nudity was nixed and Pompeana wore a white bodysuit that covered her from head to toe instead.

Other intriguing shows from that first season included a piece by the Paul Taylor Dance Company and a joint South African-American musical about women called *Sheila's Day*. There were also a few pieces that didn't go over too well, such as an absolutely God-awful opera about American football and a storytelling festival. The latter was in the wrong venue; the former was just wrong.

At the end of the season the New Victory hosted the 1996 Drama Desk Awards. As we rolled toward the summer the schedule slowed down, so Kelly, one of the house managers, arranged for some of us to interview for jobs with Shakespeare in the Park. I jumped at the chance to move on and up; I had already decided that the New Victory was going to be a stepping-stone, not a destination.

Shakespeare in the Park Delacorte Theater

Almost every night at the Delacorte Theater in Central Park, a gentle breeze blew across the lake as Andre Braugher, playing King Henry V, ripped into the "Once more unto the breach" speech. Tennis balls were scattered across the floor, and at intermission we stood in front of the stage to keep patrons from stealing them.

Before I started working on Broadway, and after my stint at the New Victory Theater, I spent one summer and fall working for the Public Theater – also with an 'er' –and their New York Shakespeare Festival. For the summer I was up in Central Park, working at the Delacorte for Shakespeare in the Park. In autumn I subbed here and there at the Public's main space on Lafayette Street in the Village. Interestingly, it was right around the block from Cooper Square and my old stomping grounds at Children's Express. CE was an international news service run by youth, and I'd worked with them until I'd aged out at nineteen.

If you're from New York City, you already know what Shakespeare in the Park is. You will have to bear with me for a moment while I explain it to our out of town friends. Every summer the Public Theater, known for premiering groundbreaking musicals such as *Hair* and *A Chorus Line*, stages two productions. Usually they're both Shakespeare plays; occasionally there's a deviation from that trend and they throw another classic or a musical into the mix. The shows go up at the Delacorte Theater, an open-air venue in the middle of Central Park.

The Delacorte is directly behind a lake and directly below Belvedere Castle, so it's a very picturesque spot. There's nothing like sitting there on a summer night, when it's warm enough to be cozy and cool enough to be comfortable, listening to someone gift you with a Shakespearean soliloquy. If you've never done it, trust me on this: it's sublime.

Tickets to Shakespeare in the Park are free. At a time when tickets to Broadway shows are prohibitively expensive for a lot of New Yorkers, that's a big deal. This might have changed, since it's been a while since I worked there, but in the late 1990s the tickets were first come, first served. You could not make reservations over the phone or online. If you wanted a ticket, you had to queue up early in the day, either at the Delacorte box office in Central Park or at the Public Theater on Lafayette Street. The lines were incredibly long; people camped out for the day on the sidewalk with blankets and lawn chairs. Some brought wine and food and made a picnic out of their wait.

The summer I worked at the Delacorte, our shows were *Henry V and Timon of Athens*. *Henry* ran from, I believe, June to July; there was a short break, and then *Timon* took over for the rest of the summer. Even though I'd taken a Shakespeare class in my senior year of high school, I'd never read those plays, so I was very interested in them.

The ushering staff was young, energetic and friendly. We flitted around the Delacorte in banana-yellow shirts. Most of us were not fond of the garish color but it served its purpose: the ushers were immediately identifiable and easy to locate. We weren't going to be mistaken for patrons, that was certain.

It was a stormy summer in New York that year. One of the production managers wore a safari hat and trench coat when it rained; she always looked like an old-time explorer from a silent film. Even if there was a storm in the forecast, the general philosophy was to try to go forward with the evening's

Belvedere Castle in Central Park, which overlooks the Delacorte.

performance anyway. Light drizzle wasn't enough to stop the show; the actors doggedly kept going. It was up to the audience to figure out how to stay dry. If and when the rain worsened, though, the performers were signaled to stop and left the stage. The patrons bolted for the covered sections of the theater and huddled together; the ushers usually joined them.

Generally, the production team tried to wait it out. If the storm did pass through, the crew wiped down the stage, the actors returned, and the action picked up where it had left off. The show wasn't completely canceled unless it appeared that the rainstorm was going to be heavy, was going to last for a while, had thunder and lightning, or was otherwise going to create a dangerous working environment for the actors. Several performances of *Henry V*, including the opening night, ended up getting canceled due to inclement weather. August wasn't quite as wet as June and July, so *Timon* had better luck.

Only half of the ushers got to stay for the entire show; the rest of us left after intermission. It was based on seniority, so I was part of the half-show crew. I didn't mind too much; it allowed me to get home before midnight. The Public took safety very seriously, and they always arranged for us to walk in groups or have security escorts out of the park. My bus stop was right on Central Park West, and someone usually stayed with me until the bus pulled up and I had safely boarded. Still, I felt better walking through Central Park when it was a little earlier in the evening.

I got to know my colleagues on these walks; on these waits. We would slump on the wooden benches outside the park and chat. One of my co-workers was reading *Great Expectations*; as he traveled through the book I checked in with him from time to time to see what he thought. He told me about the angry notes to Pip he was writing in the margins; I confessed that I'd felt similarly and had really hated Pip after a while. On other nights the conversations veered toward sex, music, or the world around us.

I worked to be a good usher, but unfortunately, most of my colleagues only remembered how drunk I got at the opening night party for *Henry V*. It was totally out of character for me, because I had pretty much grown out of drinking altogether by the time I was seventeen years old. Even before then I hadn't particularly been out of control. I'd gone to a lot of rock clubs as a high school student, and I'd had no trouble getting served at the bar – odd, since I didn't look anywhere near twenty-one and I never had a fake ID – but I'd usually ordered one mixed drink, sipped it all night, and left it at that. Most of the time I just got soda, anyway; it was cheaper and tasted better. I certainly didn't engage in the drinking and partying that everyone expected of university students. I didn't live in a dorm, I didn't attend a party school, and frankly I had neither the time nor the inclination for that. Getting trashed wasn't my style. I didn't judge those who chose to partake; I just didn't find being inebriated to be very much fun.

It happened this time, though. I was used to drinking vodka and whiskey in mixed drinks. They served Bailey's at the party, and it was completely unfamiliar to me. I was drawn in by the sweetness and I didn't realize how strong it was. Considering that a single beer was enough to intoxicate me, drinking multiple glasses of Bailey's turned out to be a very bad idea, and before I knew it, I was asking people about their shoelaces. I didn't puke, I didn't dance on a table and I didn't sleep with anyone, but if you talked to me you immediately knew I wasn't sober.

Thankfully, I wasn't the only employee who had gotten wasted. The house manager finally herded us all together, put us in cabs with escorts, and sent us home. The next morning I called them to apologize, and when I showed up for work that night, they greeted me by pretending to stumble around.

I wasn't at my best for the *Timon of Athens* opening night, either. During one of the first previews I became feverish midway through Act I. The house manager sent me backstage, where I rested in a hammock that had been put up near the lunch tables. When it became obvious that I was way too ill to work, he sent me home for the night. By the time I reached my apartment, red spots covered both of my arms. By the time I got to the doctor's office the next morning, I was running a 103-degree fever. I'd come down with chicken pox, the childhood disease I'd never actually had as a child. I'd had scarlet fever and Rocky Mountain spotted fever, but the more common illness had eluded me for some reason. I never said I was normal.

Getting chicken pox when you're a teenager isn't particularly fun. Trust me there. The illness made me too exhausted to even rise from my couch, and the anti-viral pills I'd been prescribed didn't seem to do much. My mother had to bring food to my apartment and check on me every day. By the time the *Timon* opening party rolled around I was no longer contagious, but I was also still too drained to function with any level of competence.

It didn't mean I needed to miss the party, though. A black dress with long sleeves and a pair of magenta tights covered the lingering pox scars, and if my face was unnaturally ashen, it matched the Goth look I was sporting. I spent the entire night at the Belvedere Castle bash sitting on a wall, moving as little as possible. That, combined with my subdued nature, convinced a few people that I was partying again, but the marks that still dotted my pale face said otherwise.

Shakespeare in the Park attracted a lot of celebrities, but that didn't faze me at all. Since I was very much out of the loop with television and film, I didn't know who half the people were to begin with. That was, until the evening that Tom Hulce showed up. Hulce was a gifted actor, and he'd played my favorite composer, Wolfgang Amadeus Mozart, in one of my favorite films, *Amadeus*. We had another rain delay that night, and I looked over at him, made eye contact, and shrugged apologetically. He grinned back at me as he ducked into the covered tunnel to keep dry, and smiled again as he returned to his seat after the rain let up. For the rest of my shift I was dancing on air, and to this day I'm still kind of chuffed that the man who played Mozart smiled at me.

Oddly enough, someone on the production staff thought I was star-struck when I truly wasn't. As I climbed through the stands one day, I walked past the Public's director, George C. Wolfe, and several members of the production team. We had a full-page photo of Wolfe in our usher guidebook, and we'd all been told that we needed to learn to recognize him and say hi if we saw him. Since I was a stickler for following directions, I cheerfully said hello as I passed by.

A week or so later, I needed to go to the New Victory to pick up a check. Instead of just handing over my money, Kelly called me into her office.

"Did you run into George C. Wolfe, by any chance?" Kelly asked. For some reason, everyone always seemed to say his full name all the time.

"Yes," I said, with a shrug.

"What did you say to him?"

"I just said hello and walked away."

"It was the *way* you said hello." Kelly went on to inform me that someone on the production team had taken exception to my encounter with the Public bigwig. Curiously, instead of bringing it to my attention, they'd reported it to Kelly.

I blinked as I replayed the scene in my head. How had I said hello, precisely? Had my voice been too high pitched? Too low? Had the word been uttered too quickly or slowly? Had there been there something in my tone of voice that had seemed suspect? I'd only said *one bloody word.*

"They told us to say hello if we saw him! Was I supposed to do something else? Was I supposed to just ignore him as I walked by?" I was completely confused.

"They were asking me if you got star-struck." I was now even more bewildered. I was many things, but a star-struck fan of George C. Wolfe wasn't one of them. I really hadn't been familiar with him before I'd started working for the Public. As such, I didn't have a recording of my "hello," but I didn't think I'd uttered it with any level of admiration, much less disturbing fannish zeal.

"What? I don't know anything about him. I just said hello because we were told to do that! His photo was in the handbook!" None of it made sense to me at all.

"Okay," Kelly sighed. "I'll talk to them." She knew all about the photo of George C. Wolfe in the ushers' handbook; it had been her idea when she worked with the Public Theater.

To this day, I really don't know why my greeting caused such offense. Nobody ever brought it up again. Luckily, I was able to steer clear of the Public Powers That Be for the rest of the summer, so I didn't have to worry about perfecting my delivery of the word "hello."

Since I didn't know which production person had made such a ridiculous complaint, they all became suspect. I made sure that I only interacted with the actors and crew members who worked in the front of house from that point on. They were uniformly friendly and cordial, and they didn't see ulterior motives in the word "hello." The delightful Henry Stram, who played

Montjoy, greeted me every night as he made his entrance for Act II. I always waved back, and by the end of the summer I had a total crush on him. When the production staff passed by, however, I tried to walk the other way or divert my attention so I wouldn't even make eye contact with them.

Of the two shows I worked that summer, I found *Timon* to be the more interesting production. The original play apparently had some gaps; these were filled in and fleshed out. Henry Stram was in the cast again, playing against the incredibly gifted Michael Cumpsty. Every night I watched Timon lose his fortune and crumble onstage; every night I held my breath during the breakdown scene. To use a cliché, it was theatrical magic.

The backstage crew might have disagreed with me due to the hundreds of pounds they dragged around every night. The Victorian tables and chairs that were carried onstage were lightweight enough, but the major set element was a behemoth metal trailer. It had several rooms and was positioned in different ways depending on the scene; the actors worked both within and in front of it. The stagehands had to manually push it to each setting. At a few points in the show there were actors standing inside the trailer when the scene changed, which added even more weight to the stagehands' load. And it didn't just move once or twice; the damn thing spun all night. I didn't envy the crew at all. It was a complete turnaround from the easy time they'd had during *Henry V*, where the set pieces and props had basically consisted of a bunch of tennis balls, a steamer trunk, a cart and a chair or two.

The closing party for the Delacorte's summer season, after the final performance of *Timon*, was a small affair, held backstage in the picnic area. Someone brought a tiny kitten to the theater for some reason, and I spent most of the night playing with it.

After the party, as I walked through the auditorium to leave the Delacorte for the last time, I noticed that the stagehands were all onstage, gathered around the hated trailer. They'd spray painted rude slogans across it and they were smashing it with sledgehammers and axes. Their glee was palpable as they swung their weapons into the walls, denting the metal sheets and driving holes through them. I couldn't blame them; if I'd been forced to push around that monstrosity for several weeks, I'd have wanted to waste it too. They'd also scattered the entire cache of prop "gold nuggets" across the front of the stage.

Despite the fact that both of our Shakespeare plays had been tragedies, the summer was a comedy for me. I left laughing.

Belasco Theatre

I've been blessed to experience many things that the average Broadway fan never gets close to. I've been to opening, closing and anniversary parties; I've been backstage, under the stage and above it, too. I've hung out in Broadway dressing rooms and watched actor friends apply and remove their makeup. I've walked across stages; I've seen rehearsals. I've been to potluck lunches in theater alleys and have received numerous production gifts. I've even performed on a Broadway stage myself. I really cannot complain at all.

The one item on my theatrical bucket list that was never fulfilled was visiting David Belasco's private apartment at the Belasco Theatre.

I subbed at the Belasco for two productions, revivals of *A Doll's House* and *Follies;* and worked there as a regular for two more, *Enchanted April* and *Six Dance Lessons in Six Weeks.* During that time I had the chance to see pretty much everything in the theater except the apartment, so again, I really can't complain. However, even today, if someone offered me a chance to see that apartment, I'd probably do whatever I could to hop on a plane and get there for my tour.

When I worked at the Belasco in the early 2000s they had two phone booths. One was in the men's room, the other in the ladies'; they were full-on Clark Kent cubicles with doors and all. Even if you had no reason to use the pay phones, sitting in the booths was fun. You could close the door and shut out the noise of the world as you chatted on your cell.

The Belasco Theatre in 2014.

The Belasco, which dated to 1907, was the most exquisitely decorated theater I'd ever seen. The murals that flanked the proscenium depicted some sort of pastoral orgy scene, with fit, nude men and women frolicking in a forest clearing. The ceiling was covered with stained glass medallions; more stained glass blossomed in delicate chandeliers and large lighting features on either side of the stage. It was all authentic Tiffany work. Cherubim were carved into the rich, dark wood in the lobby. Even the door to the men's room was elaborate.

If you've ever read one of David Belasco's plays, this all makes perfect sense. If you haven't – and you really should at least pick up *The Return of Peter Grimm* – I can explain it briefly by telling you that Belasco was incredibly detailed and thorough in his set designs. There was no such thing as an insignificant set piece, prop or costume in a Belasco show. In Mary Pickford's autobiography, *Sunshine and Shadow*, she described an incident where Mr. Belasco railed on a crew member for filling a prop sugar bowl with syrup instead of molasses, even though nobody in the audience was ever going to see it. I'm sure the same exacting attention to detail was put into his theater, and that every single wall sconce and staircase newel had some specific meaning.

I'm trying to remember now. . . where were the bees? In another theater affiliated with Belasco in New York, the New Victory, the seat ends had bees on them. Bee, B for Belasco, you get it, right? There must have been bees in the Belasco Theatre too, but for some reason I don't remember where they were anymore. The next time you see a show there, check the ends of the seats for me and let me know.

Unfortunately the Belasco hadn't always been treated kindly. By the 2000s, some of the boxes had been hacked off the walls and the white seats were old and dingy. The gorgeous Tiffany medallions on the ceiling and the murals along the walls were so grimy that they were almost completely obscured. Fortunately, they were among the first elements of the theater to be restored; in 2003, a major cleaning program returned them to their former glory. The difference was drastic; once they were cleaned the medallions were so vivid that they brightened up the entire theater.

Backstage, the Belasco Theatre was built like a maze, with winding hallways. Even finding the ushers' lounge was an adventure; to get there you had to locate the right secret door to get backstage and find the correct room along a labyrinthine corridor. The room itself, with its cheerful carpeting, lockers, microwave and OSHA regulations posted on a bulletin board, seemed somewhat alien in its modernity and brightness.

The balcony was physically cut off from the rest of the theater and was accessed through a separate entrance. I've learned that during the Belasco's extensive renovations in 2010 a staircase was rerouted to connect the balcony to the rest of the house, but when I worked there it was the equivalent of Siberia. The only way for the ushers to access the balcony from the lower levels was via a

One of the beautiful Tiffany medallions on the Belasco Theatre ceiling, 2003.

secret passageway. And the stairs! I lost count of how many flights it was up to the balcony. You felt as though you'd climbed a mountain by the time you made it to the top.

Being sent to the balcony was a lonely fate. It was so quiet and so remote. I was relieved when I had a partner working with me, because being up there alone was a little spooky. I was grateful that the lighting booth was located there too, because it meant that a few stagehands were always present. One perk of the section, though, was its close proximity to the Tiffany medallions embedded in the ceiling. Whenever I was assigned to the balcony I spent a considerable period of time gazing up at the stained glass and trying to decipher the symbols on the crests. I think I may have even voluntarily trekked upstairs once or twice to study the medallions.

I always looked for the cat. He never had an official name, but everyone knew him. A few folks called him David, after our theater's namesake. He was a huge, scrappy black and white feral who lived in the alley by the stage door, and several people took up the task of feeding him. He had a lovely cat house that shielded him from the elements, provided by Rosie Perez, who performed at the Belasco in *Frankie and Johnny in the Clair de Lune*. The Belasco Kitty generally made himself scarce when people were about, but every now and then you caught a glimpse of his big yellow eyes glittering in the back of the alley.

For a few weeks there was a dog at the Belasco to go with the cat, but she was a major nuisance. She belonged to Jane Adams, who briefly came into *Enchanted April* at the end of the run, after Molly Ringwald and Isabel Keating had both left the show. I have no idea how Adams got on with the cast and crew, but the ushers couldn't stand her, either on or offstage. We didn't care for her dog either, because it ran around backstage unleashed, unattended and uncontrolled. It wasn't entirely unheard of for performers to bring their dogs to work, but they were generally very responsible about it. The dogs stayed in the dressing room or with their owners at all times, and you didn't even know they were there. An actress who let her dog run amok and roam the theater wasn't the norm, and it wasn't appreciated at all.

I was severely allergic to dogs and had landed in the ER in the past when I'd come into contact with them, so while the

The Belasco Cat in a rare public appearance.

Adams hound was on the loose I had to watch my back backstage. After the dog came into the ushers' room, stole someone's lunch and scattered the debris across the carpet, our chief had to speak to the house manager about it. Some ushers were on very limited incomes; when they bought so much as a bagel it had to be budgeted out. If someone stole their food they couldn't necessarily afford to replace it. Jane Adams certainly didn't care about that. As far as I know she never even apologized, much less offered to replace the meal that her dog had destroyed, so an usher might have gone hungry that day.

Aside from Adams, we were very fond of the *Enchanted April* cast. Jayne Atkinson was an absolutely lovely person, and the rest of the actors were similarly friendly when they ran into us. In the aftermath of a citywide blackout, Michael Hayden even offered the shower in his private dressing room to an usher who had spent days without power or water in the sweltering summer heat. The usher gratefully accepted.

During *Six Dance Lessons in Six Weeks*, relations between the cast and ushers were similarly warm. Mark Hamill came to the front of the house one night to give us a basket of Halloween candy and do voice impressions for us. When I went to London for my birthday, I bought a slab of Cadbury chocolate for him to return the favor. On opening night he sent us each a photo with a personalized inscription.

Life at the Belasco was good. If only the theater had been open more often, I would have stayed there indefinitely.

Between shows on matinee days I'd usually secret myself away somewhere in the theater with a good book and a bowl of soup. My favorite spot was a carpeted nook backstage between the ushers' area and the letters room, an eerie space where they stored all of the gigantic illuminated letters that were used on the marquee. The letters were nearly as large as I was; picking them up must have required heavy equipment. If I continued down the corridor and turned a few corners, I found myself in the large space that housed David Belasco's swimming pool. The pool itself was still there, albeit stripped of all decoration; there was enough space around it to host quite a gathering.

There was one staircase I knew about that went up to David Belasco's private apartment. Belasco had resided there from 1910 onward, surrounded by books, antiques and art. Oh, how I wanted to see it. I would stand at the bottom of that stairway and gaze up with fierce longing. Although I'd been into numerous "secret" theater apartments, including the ones at the Lyceum and the Longacre, Belasco's was the Holy Grail for me.

I dreamt of it. I'd look up the steps toward a door I couldn't see and imagine myself opening it and walking through. On numerous occasions I thought of sneaking up on my own, but I didn't want to get fired. There wasn't any legitimate reason for me to be on the top floor of the theater, so I couldn't just pretend I'd accidentally ended up there en route to somewhere else. I'd been told that the apartment was rigged with alarms and motion detectors, and the entrance was probably locked, so in any case, there wasn't any way I was going to be able to mosey upstairs and sneak in without being noticed.

I knew people who had visited the Belasco apartment. They swore up and down that there wasn't much left to see. . . well, save for the loft, or the beautifully tiled fireplace, or. . . never mind. I'd seen photos, and I knew that the apartment had been stripped to the bare walls. I didn't care. I still wanted to visit. Crew members and doormen told me that they sometimes heard parties going on in the apartment; that the motion detectors picked up people who couldn't be seen on camera. I had no reason to doubt it. The Belasco Theatre was filled with energy.

Even though I never made it to the apartment, I did get to see David Belasco's private office once or twice. It was still used by the house manager, and it was located right above the box office, behind a wall of thick bottle-glass. The manager kept an autographed photograph of David in her office. Another photo hung in the lobby, presiding over the scene below. His beloved

David Belasco.

theater had been abused so many times; the least one could do was to pay him a measure of respect.

The ushers certainly respected David Belasco. He was on a first-name basis with us, and we sometimes said hello and goodbye to him. I will not repeat ghost stories about David, but I will say that everyone knew he was there with us. Was he there literally or figuratively? That was for each of us to decide for ourselves. For David's birthday one year, I printed out a birthday card with his photo. We all signed it and wired it to the gate outside the stagedoor. It wasn't the only thing affixed to the gate – David had a devoted fan that left him floral tributes on his birthday and the anniversary of his death.

David wasn't a fearsome character by any means, but a few of the ushers did approach the idea of his ghost with trepidation. To be fair, according to old-timers around the theater, the only time he'd ever seemed truly angry was during the 1970s run of *The Rocky Horror Show*, when many of the design elements of the house had been severely damaged or destroyed. You really couldn't blame the man for being furious about that. He was there to watch over his theater, and seeing it get trashed must have been extremely upsetting to him.

What would David do? I always wondered. Did he like what he saw? When I watched a performer stumble through her blocking onstage and miss her lines for what seemed like the hundredth time, I could just imagine David's reaction. Perhaps it wasn't my imagination at all. He was standing right there, wasn't he? His arms were crossed; his face was a mask of sheer disgust. *In my day, she would have been fired on the spot.* Of course. How could anyone ever doubt, even for a second, that David was in the house? It was his pride and joy. When the curtain rose for Act II of *Enchanted April* and revealed a stage completely covered in flowers, climbing vines and lush greenery, I could see David's smile: *Now, that's a set. And it's a considerable improvement over Act I.*

David kept all of us in line, I think. We were in his theater, we knew it, and we weren't about to screw up. David wouldn't have liked it.

David's birthday card from the ushers, pinned to the stage door gate.

Rent
Nederlander Theatre

The line of tents stretched all the way down to 8th Avenue, and the teenagers and young adults in the queue were bundled up in heavy coats and hats. Some of them were sitting in beach chairs on the sidewalk. Others huddled in small groups, shared food, listened to the radio, or hopped back and forth to try to keep warm. It was only about fifteen degrees Fahrenheit, but the Rentheads had been outside for hours. I was amazed that nobody had fallen to hypothermia yet.

Rent offered cheap tickets for seats in the first two rows of the orchestra. After the show had been open for a while these tickets were sold by lottery, but at the beginning of the run they were first come-first serve. Ardent fans queued up very, very early to get them. I was told that the tent city appeared every night as fans camped out on 41st Street to be first in line for tickets the next day. Even though I thought it was perhaps *slightly* overzealous, I had to admire these superfans' commitment to their favorite show. The Rentheads stood their ground in the freezing January night even though they had already seen the show multiple times; they were dressed as their favorite characters and knew every lyric and bit of dialogue.

I wasn't a Renthead. However, when I was sent over to the Nederlander to sub for one performance of *Rent*, I was excited for three reasons. One, it was a new show. Two, I'd never been to the Nederlander Theatre. It was an incredibly ramshackle, run-down house, and I loved those.

Three: ushering was the only way I was going to stay warm at night. The heat in my apartment building had broken down a week earlier, my home was freezing cold, and thus far, my landlord had completely ignored the entire situation. Even worse: the spring term at my Uni hadn't started yet, so I didn't have anywhere warm to go during the day. With no other recourse, I bundled up in multiple layers of sweaters and gloves when I was in my icy apartment, and tried to spend as much time as possible in places that offered central heating, like the library. Working as an usher provided me with another temporary refuge from the cold.

However, my zeal fizzled shortly after I walked into the ushers' room at the Nederlander Theatre and discovered that I was going to be treated like shit all night long. The ushers were on par with the rudest patrons I'd ever seated. I was sent up to the mezzanine, where one of the regulars said exactly three words to me: "You. Over there." It wasn't an auspicious beginning.

I didn't enjoy the show at all. Idina Menzel as Maureen was brilliant, but she was the only bright point for me. To make matters worse, I was horribly cold, because the old theater was drafty. I usually wore nice black sweaters to work in the winter, but I wasn't permitted to do that at the Nederlander. *Rent*'s ushers were supposed to look less formal than traditional Broadway staff, so I had to go on the aisle in a short-sleeved black t-shirt. I didn't even have an ushers' scarf or collar around my neck to provide a little extra warmth; I had to wear a *Rent* sticker instead. As I watched the show I shivered, longed desperately for the toasty sweater I'd been forced to leave in the ushers' room, and rubbed my arms to try to keep warm.

I was in college full time, working full time, and living in an unheated apartment. And there I was, watching a bunch of pretentious losers sing about how wonderful it was not to pay rent and how it was selling out to work. I found myself soured on the show by the end of the first act. This was my generation? Really? These were the people with whom I was supposed to identify? Anyone who thought that those of us on the cusp of Gen X and Y behaved this way en masse didn't have a fucking clue. I had nothing in common with those pompous transplants.

Yeah, I was bitter. I'll freely admit it in this case.

As I ventured out into the frosty evening after the walk-out, bundled up in several layers of clothing, I pulled my scarf tight around my face. To say that I had not been converted to the Church of *Rent* would be an understatement. I looked back one last time at the line of tents and lawn chairs, which had grown significantly during the three and a half hours I'd been working, and I shook my head. It boggled my mind to know that I had what the Rentheads wanted more than anything: I'd seen the show that night. In fact, I'd been paid to see it. I knew that any of the fans in that queue probably would have traded places with me in two seconds flat, and that it would have been a brilliant and fulfilling experience for them. One woman's trash is another's treasure, as they say. I tried to remind myself of that little fact as I headed off to the bus stop.

When I returned to the Nederlander Theatre the next week to pick up my check, it wasn't there. The people at the box office were snippy when I asked if they could please double check for me, and I was finally told that I would need to wait around to talk to the head usher. Since I needed to get to work at another theater on time, I declined and left. And since the Nederlander was all the way down on 41st and I usually worked further uptown, I never bothered to go back. I needed the money desperately, but I honestly didn't want to deal with anyone at *Rent* ever again. I knew that the theater was supposed to mail my check at the end of the week if I didn't pick it up in person, so I figured I'd just have a short delay in receiving my pay.

My check arrived in the mail several months later. The envelope was dirty, there was a shoeprint across the address, and it was covered in coffee cup rings and brown stains. I wouldn't have expected any less. It was a fitting finale to my *Rent* experience.

Chicago
Shubert and Ambassador Theatres

The Broadway revival of *Chicago* has been in three different theaters since it started its run in 1996. It began at the Richard Rodgers on 46th Street, moved over to the Sam S. Shubert on 44th, and finally bounced up to the Ambassador on 49th, where it remains to this day. It's now in its 19th year, it has surpassed *Cats* as the second-longest running Broadway show, and from what I understand, it's not planning to go away any time soon.

I subbed at *Chicago* many times. During the first spring I worked for the Shuberts, the original cast members – Bebe Neuwirth as Velma Kelly, Ann Reinking as Roxie Hart, Joel Grey as Amos Hart and James Naughton as Billy Flynn— were still with the show. Bebe returned at least once later on to reprise her role as Velma, and I was always glad to see her name in the program.

Bebe is one of the nicest, most gracious, most fantabulous Broadway performers I've ever had the pleasure to meet. I will go on record with that.

I seated Bebe at several opening night performances for other shows. She always looked me in the eye, smiled and said hello as she handed over her ticket. Most patrons didn't do that even at regular performances. On an opening night, when many audience members treated the ushers like pond scum, it was truly an anomaly. At one show, after I took her to her seat I turned around to see her picking her way through an empty row. I was baffled until I realized that even though she needed to get to the lobby, she hadn't wanted to block my aisle or get in the way of all the other patrons I was seating. Celebrity or not, most people aren't even remotely that considerate. Bebe always was.

Other than those brief opening night greetings, I never had a chance to chat with Bebe. When I subbed at *Chicago* I saw her onstage as Velma Kelly; every now and then when I was crossing through Shubert Alley after an evening show I caught a glimpse of her at the stage door, surrounded by enthusiastic fans.

One weekend when I was subbing at *Chicago* there was a new Roxie Hart. The actress, who shall remain nameless in the interest of kindness, had a beautiful operatic voice. Unfortunately, that didn't work very well in *Chicago*. I think that if she had been doing a different sort of show – *Show Boat*, perhaps; *The Phantom of the Opera*, *Les Mis*, a Rodgers and Hammerstein piece – she would have brought down the house. As Roxie, however, she was totally out of her element. The songs weren't right for her voice, the interaction with the audience seemed to make her uneasy, and it was obvious that she hadn't yet become comfortable with the choreography.

Usually when a performer crashes and burns it's juicy gossip both backstage and in the front of the house. In this case, however, nobody mocked our hapless Roxie. Everyone seemed to be aware that she was doing the best she possibly could and was just perhaps in the wrong venue; an Olympic gold medalist diver forced to perform on a ski slope, so to speak.

Before the matinee I sat on my aisle arranging my Playbills. The usual pre-set din provided accompaniment to my work; musicians tuning up, stagehands walking back and forth. I knew without looking at the stage that Bebe, who was back in the show as Velma, was out there too. She always was. Before half-hour you tended to find her onstage doing a focused ballet barre.

This particular afternoon, however, it sounded as though a dance class was underway. I stood up and looked toward the stage to see what was going on.

"No! Don't do it that way, you will hurt your knees!"

Bebe was onstage in her leotard, as usual. However, instead of doing pliés, she was coaching the new actress. The two of them were running through Roxie's choreography, and Bebe was giving her co-star pointer after pointer. Not only was she trying to make sure that the new Roxie knew the dances, she was trying to ensure that they were performed safely.

How many leading actresses would have done what Bebe did? It would have been very easy to sit back, shrug, and say, "It's not my problem. Let the dance captain handle it." A lesser actress might have been happy to see her co-star struggle and fail.

Not Bebe. She was invested in the success of the show as a whole, not just herself. She cared about her colleagues. She clearly wanted the new girl to do well, and she was even willing to sacrifice her own time to make that happen.

And that, friends, is why Bebe Neuwirth is the kindest, most wonderful Broadway performer of all.

I don't think I'd ever be inclined to join a Broadway performer's fan club. If I did, though, it would be Bebe's. (Jazz) hands down.

Copenhagen
Royale Theatre

Everything we call real is made of things that cannot be regarded as real. If quantum mechanics hasn't profoundly shocked you, you haven't understood it yet. – **Niels Bohr**

The stage seats at *Copenhagen* were situated in a gallery high above the white circle of the set. During the show the audience members looked down on the action like arbiters or, perhaps, angels. Given that all three of the characters in the play were supposed to be dead, either or both of those possibilities would have been plausible.

I always got a kick out of stage seating. I'd first encountered it at *Cats*, and when I'd seen the show as a patron it had been my location of choice. Becoming part of the action appealed to me; I liked being up close and personal with the performers.

Set designers had become very clever with their stage seating configurations, too. At *Inherit the Wind*, the action took place in a courtroom. The audience stage seats made up the jury box and spectator gallery, and the actors were scattered amongst the patrons. I never worked at *The Annual Putnam County Spelling Bee*, but I heard that some lucky audience members there were active participants in the show: they sat on the bleachers with the actors and actually spoke. The stage seats at *Copenhagen* were far less participatory, but no less critical to the overall impact of the set design.

For the cast, crew and front of house staff, stage seating always required special vigilance. It was an arrangement that could turn very bad very quickly if an audience member got up and wandered onto the set, found their way backstage, or dropped something from the seating gallery to the stage. For this reason, most productions with onstage seating stationed at least one usher in the wings to monitor the patrons.

At *Inherit the Wind*, patrons sitting in the onstage jury boxes were required to leave their belongings in lockers backstage to ensure that nothing ended up on the set. I heard that the same was done over at *Spring Awakening*. Nothing so drastic happened at *Copenhagen*, but every single onstage patron was warned that they could not leave their seats once the performance started. We begged and pleaded with those guests to please, please, use the restroom before the show, get that drink of water *now*, and take care of all phone calls before going up to the gallery. Most of the time they were smart enough to take us seriously.

Once the show began we sat in the wings, strategically positioned at the bottom of the staircases to the galleries. Nobody could get past us. We couldn't go anywhere either, since we were bound by the same restrictions as the patrons. At intermission there was a changing of the guard, and two different ushers came onstage to patrol the wings until the end of the performance.

I subbed at *Copenhagen* on a fairly frequent basis. It was a fictional straight play that speculated on the real-life 1941 meeting between the brilliant German scientist Werner Heisenberg and his former mentor, Niels Bohr. If you've ever taken chemistry you've heard the name *Bohr* before; he designed the circular atomic model you had to draw and fill with electrons. The play was fascinating and the actors, Michael Cumpsty, Blair Brown and Phillip Bosco, were truly excellent. It wasn't light entertainment; if patrons weren't prepared to think they weren't going to enjoy themselves. I could always tell when people with science backgrounds were in the house; they laughed at the references to chemistry and physics that the rest of the audience just didn't get.

Normally, I was intrigued to go backstage at Broadway shows because I could observe all the frenetic activity that went into the production. I loved the idea of working backstage at *Copenhagen* in concept, but in reality, the experience was as inert as argon. There weren't any set changes and all three actors stayed onstage the whole time, so I didn't get to see the stagehands or dressers bustling about. After Phillip Bosco waved hello and went onstage – and he always did, kind man – there wasn't anything at all to do or see. I was trapped in a pitch black, warm space. I couldn't actually see the show from my vantage point, I could barely hear it because the theater's acoustics weren't designed with backstage in mind, and I was consequently so bored that I struggled to stay awake. I didn't dare nod off, however. I was always worried that if I wasn't paying full attention a patron might get past me, wander onto the set, and disrupt the play. The only thing left to do was to sit numbly in my chair and watch the actors' shadows dance across the bare brick walls. It was my own personal shadow-puppet show, I guess.

I wasn't the only one who found the backstage shift to be ineffably tedious. Toward the end of Act II there was an atomic bomb sound effect. The ushers always joked that it was their alarm clock; it woke everyone right up again. That says it all.

One weekend when I had a major chest infection I was assigned backstage. It was a job that none of the regulars wanted to do so they relegated it to the subs when they could; they knew that I was savvy enough to handle it responsibly. Knowing that every sound I made would carry to the stage, I struggled to keep myself from coughing or clearing my throat. On the rare occasions when the silence was interrupted by laughter or applause from the audience, I took the opportunity to cough as much as I could. When I couldn't stop myself from coughing at other points in the show, I pressed my face into a cushion to muffle the sound.

It was impossible to read backstage at *Copenhagen*, but once someone tried, or so I heard. A sub brought reading material with her to the backstage post. Since it was too dark to see, she angled her chair toward the stage to get some light. And then she scooted over a little more. And a little more. And suddenly the audience was treated to the vision of an elderly woman sitting on the edge of the set, reading. She was oblivious to the ushers and house manager in the orchestra, who frantically tried to gesture to her to move back into the wings, so someone had to go around through the stage door and yank her offstage.

The first line of the show was "Why did you come to Copenhagen?" I'm sure everyone who saw that poor elderly usher was wondering just that.

The Invention of Love
Lyceum Theatre

Denise: Tickets please?
Patron *(angrily):* Of course I have a ticket! How do you think I got in?! *(storms away)*
Denise *(aside):* On your broom, perhaps?

If I had to choose the worst show I ever worked, it would be *The Invention of Love* at the Lyceum.

The irony is that on paper, it should have been a very positive experience. The production team was fabulous and always included the ushers in activities and parties. We adored the actors, and they liked us in return. One of the leads, Richard Easton, even thanked the front of house staff when he won a major award for his performance in the play. I didn't think the play itself was particularly well-written, but the actors slayed it and the set design was gorgeous. There was one scene in Act II, where the protagonist watched fireworks from a hill in the English countryside, which was breathtakingly beautiful.

The other ushers were awesome, and I genuinely enjoyed all of them. We greeted each other with hugs and laughed as much as we could. My dear friend Greg was at the Lyceum with me, and we were lucky enough to be assigned as aisle partners for the entire run. The ushers' room was large and comfortable.

The Lyceum Theatre itself is a beautiful 1903 Beaux-Arts jewel box; it is tied with the New Amsterdam as the oldest currently operating Broadway house. Technically, the New Victory is slightly older than both venues, but since it was designated as an off-Broadway theater when it reopened, it's not counted. The Lyceum also holds the record as the oldest Broadway theater to operate continuously. Unlike both the New Amsterdam and the New Victory, it's remained a legitimate house for a full century, and has never switched to films or closed down. There is an elaborate, but disused, smoking room downstairs with warm, rich carved wooden walls. A goddess presides over the proscenium. The Lyceum also serves as a mini-museum of sorts: it houses the Shubert Archives, a repository of historical documents, images and artifacts pertaining to Broadway. Photos of theatrical stars line the lobby and central staircase. Long story short, it's a beautiful and intriguing theater.

What made *The Invention of Love* so horrible, then? The audience. Hands down, no question, the audience. The audiences that came to *Invention* were downright ghastly. They were rude, they were snappy, they were pompous, and they acted as though we were the enemy.

After a while, that is just what they became.

We inwardly cringed every time the ticket taker yelled, "The house is open!" I began repeating the "Once more unto the breach" speech from *Henry V* to steel myself each day. We hummed the Wicked Witch of the West's theme song from *The Wizard of Oz* when especially horrid patrons walked away. We tried to smile, but when were being abused at every single performance for no reason at all, our spirits invariably flagged.

Not a day passed when there wasn't an audience/usher conflict at the Lyceum during *The Invention of Love*. Many patrons were angry and hostile from the moment they walked into the building. They yelled at us because the theater was old, the mezzanine was small, and the balcony was high up. It was our fault that there were not enough stalls in the restrooms. An elderly man told me that the "rotten old theater" should be torn down. Numerous guests became ornery when I told them that they couldn't put their feet up on the ancient metal radiators on the mezzanine landing. They weren't just complaining or making observations; they seemed to be accusing of us of personally designing the theater to thwart and frustrate them.

It reached nightmarish proportions very quickly. People tried to snatch Playbills from my hands and pushed me out of the way. They screamed at me when I would not let them walk on the fire escapes. They were even livid when we asked for their tickets so we could figure out where they were sitting. That was a biggie; it happened every single day. It defied logic, really: in order to seat them we needed to know their exact locations. In order to know their exact locations we needed to see the tickets. Patrons didn't get this, however, and they acted as though we were asking for their firstborn children when we requested to see their ticket stubs. I

Greg and I were probably smiling because there weren't any patrons around.

guess they thought we could figure out where they were sitting through our special psychic powers.

One woman proclaimed that I was "really stupid." Someone argued with Greg and me because the house did not open to the public until half-hour. Early in the run, management had to position two ushers right next to the stage during intermission because patrons kept hurting the floor microphones and stealing the prop leaves that were scattered across the set.

Some patrons actually got physical with us. One of my colleagues was poked in the back. Old men believed it was appropriate to try to stroke my arms or shoulders and were offended when I pulled away. On one occasion someone grabbed me by the shirt and yanked so hard that the cloth stretched out. Many customers seemed to have a problem grasping the concept of personal space.

At the conclusion of one particular matinee two women refused to leave the theater, which meant that *I* could not leave. When I gently asked them to please move toward the lobby after I'd watched them walk in circles in the empty orchestra section for several minutes, one of them got in my face and screamed, "I want a New York experience!" I am still not quite sure why perambulating in a loop for ten minutes was more of a "New York experience" than seeing the play or, I don't know, actually *walking around New York*, but hey, what do I know.

On another day a colleague and I had to contend with a man who had a conniption because we wouldn't let him go through the passdoor, the passageway that connects backstage to the front of house. Why this was such an issue? People who are not in the production or associated with the theater in some way are *never* allowed to walk through the passdoor, or anywhere backstage, without an escort that personally knows who they are. It's a very strict security rule. There wasn't anyone in the house to meet this man and nobody was scheduled to do so, but he honestly thought we should endanger every single actor, crew member and house staff member by letting him walk around backstage unattended. Taking a two-minute walk to the stage door was beneath him. He was red with rage by the end of the exchange; his wife, who was standing to the side with her head in her hands, was visibly mortified. The stage manager finally appeared to rescue us; later in the day she apologized for the incident.

The fact that the ushers, actors and production staff enjoyed each others' company really kept us all sane. On the first day of the show Jeff Weiss, who played Charon, the boatman of Hades, met me at the stage door. He welcomed me to the Lyceum as though he were welcoming me to his home, and in a way, he was. I adored Jeff, and whenever I ran into him I knew I was in for a lively, fascinating conversation. I also enjoyed chatting with David Harbour, who played Moses John Jackson. His character was an athlete, and he jogged around backstage and did exercises to make himself legitimately sweaty. Every now and then my break coincided with his evening laps, and he'd stop for a moment to talk.

There was a foam wig head in the ushers' room. Nobody claimed it and it didn't seem to actually belong to Wardrobe, so we decided to have fun with it. Greg and I named him Hermie and did him up with lipstick, stringy hair and a hat. Hermie lived in our lounge for a while, but at some point he was spirited away to parts unknown, never to be seen again.

As the months passed we developed as many coping strategies as we could. The first was to walk away from irate patrons – those who were simply arguing for the sake of arguing, and didn't actually need anything – to breathe and defuse the situation. Some guests calmed down or ran out of steam when they realized they didn't have someone to harangue anymore. If they legitimately required help we would summon the assistance they needed, get away from them as quickly as possible, take a deep breath and stroll around the lobby for a few minutes to regroup before returning to our posts.

The second coping strategy was to laugh as much as we could. We shared our war stories, and they reminded us all that

The irrepressible Jeff Weiss.

we weren't alone in our strange, hostile world. Everyone sharpened their storytelling skills as they regaled their colleagues with lurid tales of the patrons with whom they'd contended the night before.

To this day I am not sure why *The Invention of Love* attracted such an ornery crowd. I'd never seen anything like it before, and I never saw it again afterward. Was it because it was a play and not a musical? Was it the subscription audience? Was it because a lot of the patrons were seniors? I don't think any of those excuses applied. During my time as an usher I worked at a lot of straight plays, a lot of shows that attracted older patrons, and a number of other productions for the Roundabout, Lincoln Center and the Manhattan Theatre Club, and none of them were as horrendous as *Invention*. Was it the subject matter? Love stories? Ancient Roman poets or Oxford scholars? A. E. Housman? England? I can't find any matches there, either. I'll perhaps never know what compelled some of the meanest theatergoers in New

York to converge at *Invention* every night, but converge they did.

But Mrs. Lincoln, how was the play? The play was, in my opinion, terrible, especially in the second act. To give it its due, it started off with what was truly a compelling story of sexual awakening and unrequited love, but by the middle of Act II it veered totally off course with random characters that came onstage to pontificate.

However, it had a wonderful safeguard against bad reviews: it made generous use of Latin. Characters in the show studied Classics at Oxford and quoted ancient Roman poets. There were also many references to Victorian-era politics, history and literature, and that threw the audience off. They thought that if they hated the show or didn't recognize every single historical character it meant that they didn't understand it. Nothing of the sort was happening; they were just seeing the Emperor's New Clothes, and they weren't confident enough to realize it.

I was often asked, "Do you understand the show?" Frequently, the query was dripping with condescension. When I answered in the affirmative, the response was generally an incredulous "Really?" I'd suddenly become the three year old who could do calculus. Since I was only a lowly usher, I couldn't possibly have the education or intellect to comprehend Catullus or the social engineering of Victorian England, could I?

They never got that it wasn't even *about* Catullus or any of the other random historical figures. It was about a brilliant poet who stuffed up his finals at Oxford; became a clerk; suffered unrequited love toward his good school friend; revealed his secret in an emotional scene with said friend; was all bogged down, repressed and restricted from showing his true colors by Victorian sensibilities on homosexuality; and finally became a nasty, irascible professor. It was a commentary on wasted potential, homophobia's ability to wreck people's lives, and general attitudes toward sexuality in Victorian and Edwardian society. Oh, and Oscar Wilde showed up, clad in purple velvet, as a counterpoint to the repressed A. E. Housman. To boot, Daniel Davis, better known as Niles the butler on the TV sitcom *The Nanny,* played Wilde.

My secret amusement toward the end of the Pompous Ancient Roman Poet Show was to learn to swear in Latin. I never said anything that would have gotten me fired if I'd said it in English, mind you. All the same, I did devise a rather brilliant rude Roman lexicon and I repeated selected phrases as I walked away from patrons who behaved like arrogant fools.

Not a single person – certainly, none of the ones who loudly proclaimed that they'd read ancient Roman poetry in the original Latin and knew far more than a plebeian like me – ever understood a word I said. What makes this even more hilarious is that there's a fair amount of profanity and slang in Catullus's work. If you've actually read him, you know that.

These *stultissima* didn't understand the easy, polite phrases, either. Really, if you claim to have studied Latin and the meaning of something like "nescio quid dicas" *("I don't know what you're talking about")* or "carpe noctem" *("seize the night")* eludes you, chances are good that you're a liar.

There's a certain savage satisfaction in realizing that the pompous windbags around you are really entirely clueless.

Def Poetry Jam
Longacre Theatre

One of the show posters lurking in my closet is from *Def Poetry Jam*, which played at the Longacre Theatre during the 2002 – 2003 season. It's covered with personal messages from most of the performers in the cast. Beau Sia wrote, "Without you I'd feel like an unpopular poet." Georgia Me admonished me to "Keep God first." Reading over those Sharpie inscriptions always makes me smile, because *Def Poetry Jam* was a participatory event for me.

I was sent over to the Longacre after my show at the Royale closed. It was a happy arrangement; I was very fond of the chief and most of the staff. I'd subbed there before for *The Young Man from Atlanta* and *Judgment at Nuremberg*, and had worked the entire run of *One Mo' Time*, which had only been about five weeks.

That was par for the course for the poor Longacre, sadly. Despite the "long" name, most of the shows that ran there were short-lived. Once they even had a production that closed after a single official performance: *The Oldest Living Confederate Widow Tells All*. The actors who appeared at the Longacre were outstanding, but the theater itself was Teflon: nothing stuck to it.

Despite all of this, we had great expectations for *Def Poetry Jam*. It brought in a different crowd than the usual Broadway show; they were young, energetic and friendly. On occasion they came in wearing sandwich boards or holding the signs they'd used to protest earlier in the day. Mixed among them were the traditional Broadway matinee ladies, teenagers and children.

Def Poetry was very much a New York show with a New York audience; we didn't tend to get a lot of tourists. It's a shame, because I think they would have loved if they'd given it a try. On the other hand, if they were looking for a traditional Broadway musical or a classic play, they weren't going to find it at the Longacre.

An onstage DJ provided music both before and during the show, so we seated patrons to the beats of 50 Cent, Ludacris, Lauryn Hill and Jill Scott. The poets in the show, who were heavy hitters from Russell Simmons' HBO program of the same name, presented both solo and group pieces. We all tried to avoid taking breaks when our favorites were on.

There's an inevitability when you work at the same show every night: you begin to learn the dialogue. There's something to be said for repetition; when you hear the same thing over and over again it burns itself into your brain, even if you're not paying close attention to it. If you talk to any regular usher at a long-running production it's entirely likely that they will be able to recite complete scenes for you, recreate the blocking and do some of the choreography. If the production ever needed backup stage managers to supervise rehearsals and prompt the actors, all they would need to do is go to the front of house. Ushers might even respond to completely random comments with lines from their show. At *Phantom*, for instance, Erik's frenzied "Don't gooooo! So BE IT!" rant from the end of "Wishing You Were Somehow Here Again" and Monsieur André's "These things do happen" comment tended to pop up a lot.

At *Def Poetry Jam* the same held true: in no time at all, we started reciting bits and pieces of the poems and working them into our conversations, completely out of context. Beau Sia's piece about "extreme" situations and Suheir Hammad's frequently reprised "Even. Now." were front of house fan favorites.

However, things went one step further than they normally did. Instead of just repeating the poems from the show, several ushers began drafting parodies of them. Perhaps, surrounded by so many brilliant and creative people, we were inspired. Perhaps we were bored. Whatever the case, almost every piece in the show eventually had a satirical version.

Our poems were about the ushering life. We lamented the conduct of a famous billionaire who had attended the show one night. We railed on latecomers and rude patrons. We borrowed Beau Sia's poem about stereotypes and transformed it into a piece about generalizations about ushering. There was a biting commentary on the poor hygiene habits of one of our colleagues, riffed from Georgia Me's "Sister 2 Sister." Poetri's ode to Krispy Kreme donuts was reworked as a love note to Popeye's Chicken, a favorite lunch choice of many of our ushers. There were only a few poems we didn't touch, mostly because they were just too serious to parody. For instance, even though we loved Staceyann Chin, none of us felt right about sending up her brutal, stirring piece on homophobia and violence. It was left alone out of respect.

The ushers' room became a rehearsal hall as we ripped through our poems. Jasmine, an usher who was a TV actress and singer, took on the role of stage manager and put together a call book. A running order was worked out. We had no idea what we were going to do with it, but it was a blast. People started showing up way before call time to recite their poems.

The cast got wind of our antics, and it opened a door to dialogue between the performers and the ushers. There hadn't been much interaction between the front and back of house, but once they discovered that we had satirized half of their show, we became friends.

Eventually someone arranged for us to perform our production, now entitled *Def Ushers' Slam*, onstage at the Longacre. I was reeling. Performing my own writing, even if it happened to be a satire of someone else's work, was an intoxicating prospect. Doing it on a Broadway stage? Even better.

The entire cast of poets, as well as some of the production team, box office staff and stagehands, came to our performance. I heard a rumor that Russell Simmons was there, too, hanging out on one of the upper levels of the theater, but that can neither be substantiated nor denied, because I didn't see him.

We printed up programs with usher bios, like the ones that appeared for the performers in the Playbills. By this time we'd all adopted a specific poet to parody. I got Beau Sia. Georgia Me's poems were divvied up between Jasmine and a male usher, and Poetri was essayed by an older woman, Regina.

Everyone's poems were received with laughter and applause, and at the end of the show the poets were on their feet to give us a standing ovation. Usually things worked the other way around, but this time they clapped for us. After the performance, we all retired to the ushers' room for a well-deserved feast.

It's been said that poetry brings people together, helps them expand their horizons, and enables them to see more of the world around them a little more perceptively. For the poems performed at the Longacre that spring, all of those statements were spot-on.

The Def Ushers onstage at the Longacre Theatre.

Cats
Winter Garden Theatre

On the Cats *set at the Winter Garden Theatre.*

Feline Rules and Regulations

The ushers' room at the Winter Garden was high above the mezzanine in a little alcove. During *Cats* it was somewhat run down; when the theater was drastically renovated for *Mamma Mia* it received a makeover. In any case, the ushers used it only to store their belongings; it was too small, too stuffy and too remote to allow for any sort of congregating.

Even though it was dingy, during *Cats* it was an oasis for me. After I put my things away I would peer through the smudged windows down to 7th Avenue and cherish the incredible luck of getting paid to see the show. When I was subbing, if Erin told me to go to the Winter Garden Theatre it was all I could do to avoid cheering into the phone. What made *Cats* different from any other production I ever worked was that I was a genuine fan of the show.

I never was able to become a regular at *Cats*. The Winter Garden was way too popular, there wasn't a lot of turnover with the staff, and I was perhaps too far down on the totem pole. However, it was a frequent destination for me. During college I subbed there often; after *Kat and the Kings* closed I was sent over as a regular sub. I ended up working at the Winter Garden for almost two months, right until I left for postgraduate studies in South Africa. When I returned to New York on my summer break I went right back to the Winter Garden for a few more weeks. As a result, it became yet another home away from home.

Working at *Cats* involved several paradigm shifts. The caveats were as follows:

One: It's your job to help keep the actors safe. Keep all of the passageways clear for them. There shouldn't be anything in their way, including people. The *Cats* cats spent a lot of time running up and down the aisles and crawling along the parts of the set that spilled out into the seating area. During the overture they did this in nearly complete darkness, guided only by the flashing green headlights they wore. They had neither the time nor the ability to dodge obstacles in the aisles; it was our job to keep their paths clear.

Two: It's your job to keep yourself safe from the performers. The cats certainly didn't want to hurt any of us, but it was very, very dark when they were running around, and they were not necessarily able to see people until they plowed right into them. It only took one collision to teach me that I'd best plaster myself to the back wall during the overture and stay clear of the curtains.

Three: Cats enjoy soft drinks. During the overture one of the bartenders in the mezzanine always prepared two sodas and set them on the edge of the bar on napkins. They weren't for the ushers. After the overture was finished, two of the cats swung by the bar to grab their beverages before scurrying backstage again.

Four: You're going to be onstage and backstage, so get used to it. *Cats* had stage seating, so we had to escort patrons through the wings to their places. On one side of the stage the audience members couldn't get backstage proper without going by the stage doorman, so it was safe. On the other side, an usher was always positioned backstage at intermission to ensure that the patrons didn't roam into restricted areas.

We also helped guard the set. During intermission the audience was allowed to walk around onstage and explore all of John Napier's handiwork. This opportunity to explore the set up close was truly unique, but it came with its own special considerations. Numerous crew members and stage managers were positioned around the set. Several were tasked with looking after the actor playing Old Deuteronomy, who "slept" onstage. A velvet rope was placed in front of him to protect him further. Several ushers had strategic posts around the stage to provide additional coverage.

My favorite post, by far, was the tire. Someone had to sit on a tire at the lip of the stage during intermission to ensure that nobody stepped on the mountains of "garbage" that made up the *Cats* junkyard or otherwise disrupted, broke or molested the set. It meant that for fifteen minutes the ushers were literally center stage.

The drawback to being onstage during intermission was that it required a constant litany of "Please don't do that." The audience often wanted to climb, jump and play the way the cats did. I can't say that I blamed them, on some level. The set was fascinating, and when I had seen the show as a customer I'd enjoyed exploring it too. When I was a teenage patron, in fact, I may or may not have been admonished not to do pique turns down the stage. I'm keeping mum on that.

Some people took it too far, though. On at least one occasion a group of adult cosplayers showed up in their homemade leotards and wigs and tried to crawl around onstage. I often had to get people down off the stage ramps. Sometimes they tried to peel back the edges of the star trap, the little trap door set into the floor of the stage that was used during "The Awefull Battle of the Pekes and the Pollicles." Once I was horrified to see a small boy deliberately stomp his heel into one of the footlights. By the time I'd shouted at him to stop and scurried over to the ramp he had scampered back into the crowd. Luckily, despite his best efforts, he hadn't managed to break or otherwise damage the gel on the light.

We had to get the stage cleared of patrons before the cats showed up again for Act II. The stage managers always gave five and one-minute warnings over the loudspeaker before the show resumed, which helped with time management. From my vantage point on the tire I could also see the monitors that linked the performers to the conductor backstage; when he reappeared on screen it was my cue to exit. For the remainder of intermission I hung out on one of the aisles, watching for problems. I was often positioned by one of the curtains at house left, so I got to greet the cats as they crawled out into the audience.

No matter how many times I was stationed there, and no matter how much I knew that the actors were going to crawl through the curtains at some point, they always managed to startle me. And I think they enjoyed it. I know I did.

Keith, Billy and the Brotherhood of the Traveling Appendicitis

A trio of Jellicle Cats and one usher.

The longer I spent around the Winter Garden the more cast members I met. They tended to be out and about in the auditorium a lot; their physiotherapists and massage therapists set up shop in the back of the orchestra before the show. As we prepared our Playbills we'd often hear the actors groaning as the masseuse worked on the aches and pains in their backs and legs. Given that the performers spent about sixteen hours a week dancing, jumping and crawling around on their knees on a raked stage, it's no wonder that the massage therapists were always completely booked up.

Billy, who was brash and bright, played Coricopat. Not that this name meant a lot to most people. That's not a slam on him or the character by any means; the fact was that most audience members couldn't tell one cat from the next. The characters that were introduced by name during the show usually had very distinct features and costume elements that helped them stand out. Grizabella had a coat, dress and heels; the Rum Tum Tugger had MTV rock hair and a studded belt; Mistoffelees was the only black cat; Victoria was the only totally white one. The patrons recognized these characters and gave them loud cheers at the end of the show. The rest of the cats, even though they were brilliant, were harder to pick out of the crowd. There wasn't anything in the program or the show itself that explained who Cassandra, Tumblebrutus or Sillabub were; the average person would draw a blank to identify them. Cat identification skills were a good barometer to differentiate the superfans from the casual theatergoers, in fact. If an audience member actually knew their Pouncivals from their Jellylorums, it indicated that they were really into the show.

Billy's Coricopat character did have one slight advantage above some of the other chorus cats; he was a twin. His costume and makeup were identical to that of a female cat named Tantomille; the two of them spent the vast majority of the show hanging out together. The twins had a special bit during "The Moments of Happiness" at the top of the second act and most of their choreography had them dancing in sync.

I hung out backstage with Billy one day when I wasn't working and watched him do his makeup. He shared his dressing room with many of the other chorus actors and swings, and it was a huge communal place with shag carpeting, Christmas lights and board games stashed on high shelves. Each actor had his own illuminated mirror and personal section at one of the long tables; many displayed family photos and artwork in their small spaces. With only a few people in the room it was comfortable, but it must have been as claustrophobic as a packed elevator when it was fully occupied.

Billy's makeup job took him about twenty minutes. He explained to me that when cast members joined the show the makeup artist came in and gave them tutorials, but after that they were on their own. Some of the actors kept Polaroids or diagrams of their makeup taped to their mirrors to guide them. Billy's makeup design was complicated but he seemed to apply it effortlessly; he picked brushes and colorful tubes out of his cosmetics kit without even looking at them. He transformed from a human friend to a feline without even breaking his conversation with me.

One of the cats in the cast gave me his appendicitis. I'm dead serious. Yes, I know it's not contagious. I'm still convinced it was passed along. Just humor me. This dancer, who shall remain nameless for privacy, had had his appendix out while I was in South Africa doing post-graduate studies. When I returned to New York on my summer break I worked at the Winter Garden, so I saw him all the time. Two weeks after I returned to Cape Town my own appendix went, and I ended up spending three days in the hospital. I later paid it forward; shortly after I returned from South Africa I worked at *Judgment at Nuremberg* at the Longacre. Two weeks after *that*, the star of *Nuremberg*, Maximilian Schell, was relieved of his appendix. I don't know who was smacked by the Traveling Theatrical Appendicitis after Mr. Schell, but I'm sure someone was.

My favorite cast member was Keith, who played three roles: Plato, the Rumpus Cat and Macavity. Plato was a slacker of a cat who appeared in the chorus throughout the show. The Rumpus Cat appeared only once, at the very end of the "Pekes and Pollicles" number, but he got to catapult through the star trap. Macavity similarly had a minuscule amount of stage time, but unlike the Rumpus Cat, he was very important to the loose plotline of the show. During Act I he was an unseen villain who intermittently made a lot of noise to terrorize the other cats in the Jellicle junkyard. When he finally emerged in the middle of Act II, with all his ginger hair standing on end, he attempted to kidnap and assault a female cat, Demeter, successfully carried off Old Deuteronomy, and had a brawl with the two largest toms, Munkustrap and Alonzo.

Yes, I know, if you've never seen the show, this is possibly too much information for you, but there's a reason I'm bringing it up. Keith's actual personality was the polar opposite of his character's; he was sweet, laid-back, generous and kind. We conversed online sometimes, even after I went to South Africa, and whether he was coaching me on gymnastics skills – I was trying to learn to do an aerial cartwheel – or asking me about Cape Town,

Wonderful Keith, in costume as Plato.

he was always great to talk to. I brought Keith a red African mask when I returned to New York on my school break; I'd seen it in a market and it had reminded me immediately of Macavity.

On my last night at *Cats* before my flight to South Africa, Keith came through the stage door with a production window card. Signatures from the cast were scattered in gold and silver Sharpie across the black poster, and at the top, in Keith's unmistakable handwriting, were the words, "Good luck, Denise!"

I took that show poster to South Africa with me and hung it in my dorm room alongside photos of my friends and family. Whenever I felt homesick, lost or unloved, it was a huge, shiny reminder of just how much some people cared about me.

Hunting for Mistoffelees Beads

One night before the show I was walking through the orchestra when I spotted a small piece of crystal on the floor. I picked it up and turned it over and over, marveling at the way the light played off the planes of the stone. And then I gasped, because I realized that I might have just found a Mistoffelees bead.

Mr. Mistoffelees was my favorite character in *Cats* for myriad reasons. I'd crushed on at least two of the actors who played the role simply because I loved their dancing. And what dancing it was: Mistoffelees, the magical cat, had the best number in the entire show. It featured a hot, sassy solo; all pirouettes and grand jetés and jazz hands, and it culminated in turns a la seconde. The audience usually erupted into enthusiastic applause after the "conjuring turns," and by the end of the solo they were roaring. Mistoffelees tended to receive one of the largest cheers at curtain call, and the accolades were well deserved.

Mistoffelees appeared as a black and white cat for the entire show, but for his solo number his regular costume was switched out for one that was all glammy Vegas showgirl. It featured a light-up jacket covered in thousands of Austrian crystal beads. From what I heard, the jacket was heavy as hell due to the battery packs that lit it up; Mistoffelees always removed the coat before he did any strenuous choreography. The rest of the costume was bedazzled, too. Some of the crystals were sewn onto the ends of delicate strings of black tubular beads which flared out, caught the light and sparkled as Mistoffelees danced. For his grand entrance in this costume, Mistoffelees spun down to the stage on a rope as he shimmered and twinkled.

Marlene Danielle, the actress who stayed with *Cats* for its entire eighteen-year run, once mentioned the Mistoffelees beads in an article by Howard Kissel in the *Daily News*. She collected them, and her comment about them piqued my attention: "Can you imagine how much energy it takes to let these fly?" It made a lot of sense to me. How much energy *did* it take to dance so vigorously that your costume actually fell to pieces? The Mistoffelees beads weren't just about beauty; they were about the raw power of dance and the love and commitment each performer brought to the role.

Before I worked at *Cats* I'd dreamed of getting my own Mistoffelees bead one day. Just one. And now I had. I closed my hand around the bead and ran up to one of the actresses who were in the auditorium. I knew what it was, but I needed to confirm it. I approached her without a greeting and stretched my hand out.

"Excuse me," I asked breathlessly. "Is this a Mistoffelees bead?" She raised her eyebrows at me and peered into my hand. "Yes, it looks like it." I thanked her effusively and scurried away.

I kept a closer eye on Mistoffelees from then on. I usually made a point of watching his solo, but now I focused on the light around his costume. Every now and then I saw crystals pop off the outfit and disappear; they resembled tiny flashes of lightning.

Billy got wind of my fascination with the beads. One night he presented me with a crystal that had rolled to his section of the stage and promised he'd look for more for me. It wasn't an easy task. Several actors in addition to Marlene collected the beads, and when one fell there was usually a scramble to get to it.

I doubted that the cast could collect every single bead that popped off Mistoffelees' costume, and surmised that some of them had to be strewn about the set. I didn't feel comfortable going onstage between shows, but I certainly could look *around* the stage in the seating area. During the downtime between matinee and evening performances I crawled around the seats in the front of the orchestra, looking for beads that might have bounced into the crevices and cracks. There were so many places for beads to hide on the edges of the set, after all. I found crystals in the ridges of the tires, on the rims of the bottles; nestled in the folds between the ramp and the carpet. Every now and then I discovered another treasure: tiny pieces of ripped fabric from the Gumbie beetles' iridescent wings; sequins from the Siamese cat costumes from the "Growltiger's Last Stand" scene; the slim black beads that attached to the Mistoffelees crystals. I started bringing a small pillbox tin to work with me to store the beads I'd found.

I tried to scout for beads as often as I could. Everyone knew what I was doing; nobody cared one way or the other. The beads were trash once they hit the floor; if they weren't reclaimed they were going to a landfill somewhere.

"What are you *doing*?" I looked up. Julius, who played Mistoffelees, had come onstage and was peering down at me with a puzzled expression. I was in the middle of my post-matinee bead hunt, and I was on my hands and knees in the orchestra section.

"I'm looking for Mistoffelees beads," I answered. I realized too late that I had just informed Julius that I was essentially looking for pieces of his costume, but it wasn't creepy like that.

"Ah," he said, and joined me. "Most of them are scattered around here. Come on up." Once a performer had invited me, I felt comfortable going onstage. Julius and I scoured the set, crawling around by the television and the old car.

"Here, let's look in the tire!" We hopped up on the large tire, upon which Grizabella ascended to the Heaviside Layer at the end of the show, to continue the search. We found some beads stuck in the seams, but neither of us were able to jimmy them free.

"Hang on," said Julius. He hopped down from the tire, scanned the floor for a moment, and came back with a handful of long black hairpins. The actors in *Cats* used scores of pins to secure their wigs on their heads; apparently they ended up getting scattered all over the place. Julius and I worked to delicately snag the beads on the hairpins and lift them out of the tire. It was like playing a theatrical version of Operation, sans buzzers; and it was something I'd never have dared to do on my own for fear of getting in trouble.

At one point I realized how utterly, wonderfully absurd it was to be stretched out on an oversized tire on a Broadway stage, exerting such exacting effort for small crystal beads that were probably covered in dust. And then I went back to helping Julius with the excavations.

Several people crossed the stage during this procedure, including, to my recollection, the house manager. Nobody seemed a bit surprised to see an actor and an usher searching for Mistoffelees beads. At the end of our hunt, I had a lovely handful of them.

Eventually I strung most of the crystal Mistoffelees beads together. Some of the loose ones still reside in the old pillbox tin, though. Every now and then I pick them up and hold them in my palm, and I think I can still feel the energy that helped them break loose.

Are You a Cat?

Actors on Broadway tend to have more privacy and less recognition than those on television or in the movies, unless they're superstars who headline the marquees on a regular basis. Even then, they're probably far less likely to be mobbed in a supermarket than a known television actor, especially if they're outside of New York. They are shielded from the audience by makeup, wigs and stage lighting; the patrons don't have the chance to scrutinize their faces up close. Average Broadway chorus girls and boys can probably live their lives completely incognito.

The *Cats* actors were perhaps the stealthiest of all. Concealed beneath layers of feathers, faux fur, yak hair wigs and full feline makeup, it was almost impossible for the casual theatergoer to recognize them out of costume. The Playbill included a page with everyone's headshots, but it was still hard to recognize people when you were using one-inch black and white photos as your reference.

Of course, the superfans had no trouble identifying the actors. A handful of the performers, who had appeared in other high-profile productions, were well known. In particular, an actress of some standing, such as Laurie Beechman, Betty Buckley or Liz Callaway, usually played Grizabella the Glamour Cat, who sang "Memory." The three Broadway actors who appeared in the film/PBS version of *Cats* were also easy to pick out of a crowd, and had cotillions of dedicated fangirls and boys. As I recall, there were even fanfic websites about the performers from the *Cats* film. For the most part, though, *Cats* cast members seemed to be able to go about their business as quietly as they wished without ever being recognized.

Patrons still wanted autographs, regardless if they could tell who was who. Thus, almost everyone who exited the Winter Garden Theatre through the stage door after the show was greeted by a clutch of eager, bright-eyed fans brandishing Playbills and Sharpies. They'd ask all of us the same breathless question: "Excuse me, are you a cat?" If someone confirmed that they were in fact a performer and started signing Playbills, the next question was typically, "Oh! Who were you?"

Every now and then I saw a performer or two pretend that they weren't cats in order to escape without signing autographs. I'm sure they had their reasons. Maybe they were just tired. Most of them did stop to sign, though, even after matinees when they were in a hurry to get lunch, get back to their dressing rooms and perhaps nap for a little while before the evening show. The *Cats* performers were good folks, by and large.

Hey! Wait! Are you a cat? It was the same question every single night. I shook my head sadly as I said, "No, sorry, I'm not." I hated to see the disappointment that crossed the kids' faces every time I told them that I was not a performer, but there was no other answer to give. Pretending to be something I wasn't would have been beyond despicable.

"What do you do, then?" asked a woman. Her child, standing next to her, smiled up at me. This took me aback; there had never been a follow-up question to the Cat Identity Query.

"I'm just an usher," I muttered.

"Will you sign my Playbill?" she said, and offered it to me.

"But I'm just an *usher*, I'm not *in* the show. . . "

"You're a part of the show too," she said firmly, and offered me the program again.

"Sure," I stammered, turned to the *Cats* title page in the Playbill, and wrote an inscription. She smiled as I gave it back to her, as though I were Grizabella or Mistoffelees.

Just an usher. Part of the show, too.

Thank you.

On the Cats *set.*

Memory

The closing marquee sign for Cats.

Right after I left for South Africa in late February 2000, the closing notice for *Cats* was posted. If you're curious as to why closing notices are always "posted," as opposed to simply announced: there's actually a piece of paper informing the cast and crew of the closure that is tacked to the bulletin board backstage. That's also why you might occasionally hear a show person say that the notice went up. It *did* go up, literally, on the wall. Whatever else the management does, whether they hold a meeting with the staff or send emails or make phone calls or skywrite or what have you, there's always that memo, printed in stark black and white, posted backstage.

   I was crushed, but it really wasn't a surprise. We'd had a lot of bad box office numbers at the Winter Garden that winter, and there had been some nights where entire sections of the theater had been completely empty. I didn't think it was a failure by any means; I just thought *Cats* had run its course. It had been running for nearly eighteen years, just about everyone in New York who went to the theater had already seen it, and there were a lot of shiny new shows that did a good job of diverting the tourists' attention. Teens wanted to see *Rent*; families with children gravitated toward *The Lion King* or *Beauty and the Beast*; those in the market for a contemporary musical also had *The Phantom of the Opera*, *Miss Saigon*, *Jekyll and Hyde* and *Les Misérables* to choose from. For dance fans, *Fosse* was doing brisk business.

I was back in New York for my summer break in June, so I had a chance to say goodbye. I actually purchased an orchestra ticket to the show so I could see it one last time as a patron, then I ushered at *Cats* for the next two or three weeks. I worked for my entire school break; I wasn't a trust fund princess and I needed the money. I also wanted to have one last run at the Winter Garden.

On my first night back at *Cats* I waited on the steps to see Julius. As he came out into the audience for the overture, he noticed me, veered over to the staircase where I was standing, and whispered "welcome back" before enveloping me in a hug. More joyful hellos and hugs were exchanged when I ran into Keith backstage at intermission. All of my performer friends were staying with *Cats* until it closed, so I was able to see Keith terrify the audience as Macavity; witness Julius's conjuring turns as Mistoffelees and watch Billy dance in tandem with his twin as Coricopat. I was among kindred spirits on the ushering staff, too; most notably, my dear friend Greg.

Somewhere along the way, it came out that I never watched "Memory." I know this was sacrilege; "Memory" was *Cats*' signature song. It was Grizabella's big moment, delivered with a hearty dose of regret and sadness. Grizabella was the black sheep of the show, so to speak; a cat with a shady past that was alternately reviled and excluded by the other characters. "Memory" was her redemption song; by the end of it, the rest of the cats knew she deserved the privilege of going to the Heaviside Layer. Old Deuteronomy flew her up to the Heavens on a magical tire. She disappeared on a silver cloud that floated away under the ceiling, and that was that.

It was all very poetic and poignant and magical, even when you realized that it was a death scene. The Heaviside Layer was Heaven, or the afterlife. You couldn't get there without dying. When all the cats were angling to go to the Heaviside Layer, they were essentially asking to die. It was pretty macabre when you considered it in that light.

Anyway, I was not a fan of "Memory." Ballads aren't my thing as a rule; I greatly prefer high-energy dance numbers. And frankly, having grown up as an Eighties child, and having heard "Memory" played everywhere from piano recitals to shopping malls, I was over it. When I worked at *Cats,* I always went to the ushers' room to get my belongings during "Memory" if I possibly could; it meant that I avoided sitting through the damn song.

"Watch it one more time. Just once," Keith urged me. I grudgingly promised to do so, and on my last night at the Winter Garden, I sat in one of the vacant boxes and watched the entire Grizabella scene. And, although I hate to admit this, "Memory" absolutely slayed me. By the end of the scene I was bawling, and that was entirely out of character. It wasn't just the music; I think it was also the realization that I really was saying a permanent goodbye to a theater and a show I loved. I knew I was never going to sit in that box again, I was never going to guard the stage, I was never going to watch friendly cats run past me in the darkness.

Cats' final performance was originally scheduled for June 2000, but as soon as the closing was announced business picked up substantially. The producers ended up extending the show for three more months and closing it in early September instead. I wasn't there to see it; I'd had to return to school.

On the September evening when the Jellicle Cats took their final curtain call, I was in Africa. Specifically, I was in Mauritius. We had another school break, and since it was only a week long, I decided not to fly home. It was far too expensive. Instead, I booked a very cheap trip to Mauritius. It was only about four hours by plane from Cape Town and it was a tropical paradise, so apparently a lot of South Africans went there for their beach vacations. In Mauritius I was able to see the Indian Ocean for the very first time in my life.

    I didn't think that much of *Cats* on the night it closed, but the next morning I woke up and it was on my mind. I looked out over the beautiful, crystal-clear Indian Ocean and realized that it was gone. I later heard that *Cats* had been given an amazing sendoff, complete with fireworks over the Hudson River, and I was sorry I had missed it.

    One of the regular ushers at *Cats*, Pat, saved her closing night gift for me. It was a professional 8" x 10" photo of the entire cast and crew, front and back of house, assembled onstage. There were so many people on staff that they'd needed to bring in the giant Growltiger pirate ship set to fit everyone in the photo. The silver frame was engraved with the show logo and the closing date.

    Looking at the image is bittersweet because several of the people on that Growltiger ship are no longer alive. One of the performers died only a few years after the show closed. Several ushers have also passed away, including Pat. Even without the photo, though, my *Cats* memories sparkle in my mind.

Mamma Mia
Winter Garden Theatre

Ghosts of future past: walking into the Winter Garden Theatre in November 2001. Usually, going into a theater after it had been renovated was akin to meeting up with a friend who had just recovered from plastic surgery: you could see the changes, but they weren't all that drastic. Entering the Winter Garden in the fall of 2001 was much more like seeing a friend who had gone through a full-face transplant, grown out his hair, and changed his name. The shell of the theater was the same, but everything inside was radically different.

The Winter Garden was dark for a full year after *Cats* closed for a top-to-bottom renovation. I'd stopped by in the middle of the spring and had been allowed to peek into the orchestra level; at the time the entire auditorium had been gutted. Now it had all been spackled back together in a shiny new configuration. The place still had a new-paint smell.

Most of the regular ushers were gushing over the changes. Where there had been only a few stalls in the ladies' restrooms, there were now many. The signage was better. The bar at the back of the orchestra had been rebuilt with shutters, so the bartenders could count their stock during the show without disturbing anyone or being disturbed. The bar and restrooms on the mezzanine had been entirely separated from the auditorium and the designers had created a warm, lush lounge area. It wasn't hard to imagine curling up on one of the lounge's banquette seats with a good book between shows. The ushers' room upstairs had been totally renovated, too. It was still way too small for anyone to congregate there, but the room now had a thick carpet, fresh paint, new lockers and a curtained changing area.

What was most striking about the Winter Garden, 2001 edition, was the fact that it resembled. . . well. . . a normal theater. I wasn't used to that. The French doors that led from the lobby to the orchestra were still there, but the feline junkyard had been replaced by a very conventional stage, a very ordinary orchestra pit and orderly rows of seating. The only reminders of *Cats*' long-term tenure that remained were a few plaques here and there in the lobby.

I was sent over to *Mamma Mia* now and then as a sub, much as I'd been initially sent to *Cats* years earlier. My love for the staff there hadn't abated, and I was thrilled to learn that an usher I liked had been hired as one of the stage doormen. Seeing his smiling face when I reported to work was a pleasant surprise.

Mamma Mia didn't appeal to me at all. The only things I liked about it were the performers themselves and the beautiful set at the end of the second act. I was roughly the same age as the protagonists, but their world was completely alien to me. It was like *Rent* again, almost. I was looking at what was supposed to be my generation, but it just didn't compute on any level. I couldn't even begin to understand the appeal of marrying so young, and even though I actually had something in common with the character of Sophia – I'd never met my biological father either – I couldn't fathom her desire to have a complete stranger walk her down the aisle. The entire tradition of being given away baffled me to begin with. And as much as I might have enjoyed ABBA's music, I couldn't understand why anyone would ever want to pay hundreds of dollars to hear it performed in a jukebox musical. For that price, one would expect to see the real ABBA.

As one of the other ushers said, though, perhaps I was thinking too much. In their words, *Mamma Mia* was intended to be a cupcake for the soul. It was neither meant to be profound nor to make any sort of political or social statements; it was simply supposed to be fun. It wasn't *my* type of fun, but that didn't make it any less valid. I hated theater snobs, and I needed to avoid being one. I tried to keep that in mind as I cheerfully brought ABBA fan after ABBA fan to their seats. If theater was about entertainment, and *Mamma Mia's* audiences spent the night clapping, singing along and dancing in the aisles, the show was obviously effective.

My work at the Winter Garden also seemed out of place. At any other theater it would have been a regular day at the office, so to speak, and I wouldn't have thought twice about it. At the Winter Garden, though, it was bizarre that things were so normal. Since I was no longer guarding the aisles, dodging performers dressed in cat costumes, or ushering patrons to their seats backstage, I was at a loss to know what to do with myself. There were no more tires to sit on at intermission; no more Mistoffelees beads to hunt. When I saw patrons dancing in the aisles during the curtain call, I had to bite back an urge to return them to their seats. In the *Cats* days they might have collided with the performers who ran down the aisles, and I would have immediately had to pull them back. In *Mamma Mia* everyone stayed firmly onstage and it wasn't an issue.

Even sadder, I realized: I wasn't going to be ambushed at the end of intermission anymore. I closed the curtains on my side of the orchestra with dejected finality, knowing that my dancer friends weren't going to pop out from behind them at any minute.

And then I was hit with a wall of sound; a huge, overpowering crash of electric guitars, bass, drums and keyboards. I jumped straight up in the air and retreated to the side of the orchestra, holding my hands over my ears. *Mamma Mia* had the sort of sound system that one usually finds at rock concerts, and I'd been standing right by one of the massive stacks of amplifiers when the band started playing. The regular ushers stood at the back of the room and laughed at me.

    I'd been ambushed at the end of intermission. Some things just never changed at the Winter Garden.

The Phantom of the Opera
Majestic Theatre

There are different types of Broadway shows. There are the ones that are absolutely, positively obscure. The only people who remember them are those who worked there. There are the productions that are short-lived but legendary, like *Carrie* or *Frankenstein*. The fact that *Carrie* only ran for sixteen previews and five performances on Broadway, but has since been revived all over America by high schools and professional theater companies alike, almost redefines the term "cult favorite." I knew someone on Broadway that actually had the *Carrie* logo tattooed on his arm. On the other side of the coin, there are shows that have respectably long runs, win awards and are initially received enthusiastically, but subsequently drop into the abyss, only to be remembered by theater geeks.

And then there are the blockbusters. They're the shows that are part of our collective consciousness. When characters sing random lines from these shows on sitcoms, almost everyone gets it. Most people recognize some of the songs, costumes and scenery, even if they've never seen the whole thing on stage. *Annie* is one of these legends; I would say that *Grease* is another. *West Side Story*, certainly. Much of the Rodgers & Hammerstein catalogue. *Cabaret. Show Boat. Wicked. Cats*, too, since "Memory" has had its own nine (hundred) lives.

We can't forget *The Phantom of the Opera*.

As the cliché goes, *Phantom* is a cultural and theatrical phenomenon. As of 2015 the Broadway show has been open for *twenty-seven years*; the London production is even older. The last original cast members have left the show by now, but there were some who held on for over two decades. Those actors went from youth to middle age, watched children grow from infancy to their high school graduations, and outlasted the Iron Curtain, the Soviet Union, and the Reagan, Bush Sr., Clinton and Bush Jr. presidential administrations. There is one usher who has been at the Majestic since *Phantom*'s opening night; in an interview it was noted that she has seen the show over nine thousand times. Some of the actors now performing in *Phantom* weren't even born when the show opened in 1988. It has become Broadway's version of *The Mousetrap*.

There's really no way to forget about *Phantom*, either. It's parodied on TV and online, and the iconic mask appears on murals and store decorations. A national tour is still wending its way around the United States, so *Phantom* show posters sprout up now and again in various cities. It was in Las Vegas for a while.

On vacation in Los Angeles in 2006 I went to a showing of *The Nightmare Before Christmas* at El Capitan Theatre in Hollywood. During the walk-in, a musician played a classic Wurlitzer organ in front of the stage. My face began to twitch when I realized he'd segued into a medley of "Music of the Night" and "All I Ask of You" from *Phantom*. I could run, but I couldn't hide.

Phantom was the first Broadway show I worked for the Shubert Organization, as a sub in 1997. It was also the last Broadway show I worked at all, in 2010. I spent about six years as a regular with the production. Between 1997 and 2004 I also subbed at *Phantom* countless times. It had one of the largest ushering staffs on Broadway, and they always needed subs to fill in.

I also visited on several occasions as a fan. A woman who frequently took my bus knew the Phantom's makeup artist, and once she arranged for me to go backstage and meet the Phantom at the time, Howard McGillin. I didn't say much to him; I simply grinned like the star-struck idiot I was at that moment. On the way out we had a brief tour of the stage and someone snapped a photo of me standing in front of the chandelier. The same woman arranged for me to buy a *Phantom* show jacket.

It always sort of bothers me that *Phantom* is viewed as a love story by many. There's a romance between Raoul and Christine, certainly, but between Christine and the Phantom? No bueno. And yes, I know I've just incurred the wrath of the thousands of *Phantom* fangirls and boys out there, but hear me out: the man is a violent, manipulative stalker. I completely agree that at the outset he's a misunderstood, sensitive genius, but the moment he starts murdering, stalking and kidnapping people, my sympathy goes out the window. One really can't excuse that.

In the original Gaston Leroux book the Phantom is known as Erik; that name is never used in the Broadway show. Erik is far more evil villain than dashing leading man, and Christine is terrified of him. She explicitly says that she's afraid of what Erik will do to her. The Phantom's only two saving graces are his musical talent and the fact that he offers up some truly funny, sardonic comments in certain scenes.

However, he's still evil. I know that one of the themes of the show is that you should judge people by their actions and not their appearance, but the Phantom's *actions* are unequivocally heinous. In both the book and the musical the Phantom takes the "If I can't have you, no one will" tack against Christine. He stalks her, he threatens her and her loved ones, he menaces everyone else at the Opera Populaire, and he kills several people. He physically abuses Christine when he rips a necklace from her neck and throws her to the ground. In addition, he tries to alienate her from her friends, he holds her captive and he possibly gains her trust through false pretenses, since, at the beginning of the show, she thinks he's the Angel of Music that her dead father promised to send in her direction. Christine's not exactly the brightest crayon in the box.

Think about it: would you really want to bring this guy home? And no, I don't think Christine is obligated to marry or otherwise hook up with the Phantom in exchange for her voice lessons.

Certainly we can acknowledge that the Phantom's disfigurement has made his life far more difficult than most, that his hardscrabble existence has contributed to his mental and emotional instability, and that he might have been able to fully use his incredible talents if he hadn't been rejected by the world. He has a bad case of unrequited infatuation, and that's enough to make anyone sing the blues. Still, the guy is an unstable, abusive, manipulative creep. It has nothing to do with his face; to paraphrase what Christine says in one number, the infection lies in his soul. It's not that I don't like a fun villain, but I always wish that people would acknowledge that he *is* a villain as well as a victim. The latter doesn't excuse the former.

Fans of the show, at least the ones that come in costume, don't seem to give much thought to Raoul, Christine's actual love interest in the story. If you've ever read the book, you know that Raoul loses his brother during the attempt to rescue Christine from the Phantom's lair. He gives up everything, including his title as a noble, his money and his social standing, to keep his girlfriend safe at the end of the story. He's arrogant but he's never abusive, he genuinely loves Christine and vows to protect her, and he puts his money where his mouth is in that regard. Yet, he's usually the one the fangirls hate. As Javert would say, if we were in *Les Misérables* and not *The Phantom of the Opera,* the world is upside down. I suppose that, as always, the good guys are less exciting to spectators than the ones with more checkered pasts.

Anyway. When I see people who worship the Phantom, it reminds me of folks who consider Freddy Krueger or Jason Voorhees to be their heroes. I especially cringe when I see children wearing the Phantom's white mask or fedora. They're unwittingly emulating a stalker and a serial killer. It doesn't compute for me, but it obviously makes sense to others.

I subbed at the Majestic intermittently from the very beginning of my association with the Shuberts; I became a regular sub in 2004 and was hired as a permanent member of staff the following year. It was considered a very good gig to get. The Majestic, like the Winter Garden and the Imperial, was a plum theater that went from one long-running show to the next. The ushers at the Majestic didn't have to worry about their theater being closed for long stretches of time; it just didn't happen. Where other theaters often housed productions that closed within a few months, the Majestic's shows lasted for years. Before *Phantom*, *42nd Street* had been there. *42nd Street* was such a hit that when it needed to leave the Majestic to make room for *Phantom*, it didn't close. Instead, the show was transferred across 44th Street to the St. James Theatre, and the chorus girls and boys tap danced over to their new home in a press event.

Owing to its large capacity, good facilities and central location, the Majestic was often used for special events. It hosted the Tony Awards numerous times, way before I showed up. A performing arts college in the city used the theater for its graduation ceremonies every year.

The Majestic was also a frequent venue for public memorials for actors with Broadway credentials. Since there wasn't a lot of reserved seating, only a skeleton crew of ushers was required for these events; the staff members were chosen on a rotating basis. Working these daytime events was entirely voluntary, but most people liked doing them. For one thing they tended to be interesting; for another, it was extra pay. I worked a number of memorials, including the ones for Bea Arthur and Tony Randall.

Memorials were always open and free to anyone who wanted to attend, and they attracted odd crowds. Many people were genuine fans who wanted to pay their respects, but we also got a lot of professional autograph salesmen and eBayers. They were painfully obvious to spot; they were the ones that hounded us for multiple copies of the program and became ornery when we didn't comply.

The invited guests at memorials included friends, family members and former co-stars of the deceased. As usual, we just seated the celebrities, we didn't interact with them. I can't say that I met Lucie Arnaz, Rosie O'Donnell or Rue McClanahan, but they all walked past me at one memorial or another.

I was always heartened that these actors were able to get a final sendoff from Broadway. They had lived for and within the theatrical community; when they passed on they were remembered fondly and with a smile. It was also a tradition to dim the lights on the Broadway marquees for a minute to honor theater personalities who died. I never actually saw this, since it happened a few minutes before curtain.

There is an old saying that there's a broken heart for every light on Broadway. I wouldn't doubt it even a little. It's also true, though, that when beloved theatrical figures leave us, every light on Broadway loses a little of its shimmer.

A Commentary on Understudies at *Phantom*

Set to the tune of "Prima Donna" from The Phantom of the Opera, *music by Sir Andrew Lloyd Webber; lyrics by Denise Reich and James Muro.*

Prima donna, she always calls in sick!
It's pretty clear, she's never here to perform.
She always backs out when they're calling her name,
The management does not adore her.

Prima donna, she's never on the stage,
They're in a rage because she's breaching her contract,
She'll never work in this town again,
Sing prima donna, no more!

(Enter: actress who called in sick AGAIN)
Prima donna? I always have the flu,
It's really true, I had the flu, please believe me!
I only miss five or six shows every week,
It's really not a huge ordeal.
Prima donna?! My understudy's fair,
She's only there because she can wear my costume!
She should be grateful that she's got this gig,
To be a prima donna like me!

Wardrobe to the Rescue

Ever dream about being naked in public? Most people have. I can't say it's high on my nocturnal play list, but I concur that losing one's clothes in a public place is a very legitimate fear to have. A corollary fear: tearing one's clothes to the point where they're no longer functional.

It was close to half-hour and I was beginning to panic about the gaping hole in my skirt. I'd torn it accidentally and it was a ragged, sad mess. I didn't have a sewing kit on me, and even if I had, the damage was too severe to mend. The most I could hope for was to suture it together with safety pins and pray that it would hold up, or at least prevent me from flashing the patrons, for the rest of the night. The only problem was that nobody had any pins.

As I began to completely melt down, someone finally suggested checking with the Wardrobe department. If anyone had pins, it would be them. I was nervous about going backstage to an unfamiliar area, so I dragged my colleague Phil along with me.

The costume shop was an explosion of color. Lush fabric was scattered on shelves and racks; costumes were lined up in neat rows and elaborate headpieces rested on mannequin heads. If I hadn't been in a panic I would have been fascinated.

The wardrobe crew didn't bat an eyelash at the two ushers who had wandered into their domain; they simply waited for us to tell them why we were there.

"Do any of you have a safety pin?" I stammered. As they raised their eyebrows, I realized how silly the question was in the middle of this fashion wonderland. They probably had boxes and boxes of pins. They probably had stock in a pin manufacturer. "I've ripped my skirt. I don't think I can save it, so I just want to avoid flashing the audience and keep it in one piece until I get home." I lifted my hands to show them the gaping hole. It was heartbreaking, really; I liked the skirt and I wasn't happy about having to throw it away.

One of the wardrobe masters hopped down from his chair, walked over to me, asked for the skirt, and gave me a beach towel to cover myself up. Instead of pinning my skirt, he sat down at his table with a needle and thread and proceeded to repair it for me.

I was half dressed and wrapped in a beach towel in the wardrobe room of a Broadway show. That might have been situation normal for the actors, who were perhaps well accustomed to making quick changes in the wings, but for me it was a whole new world. Phil and I laughed with the wardrobe master as his hands danced across the fabric of my skirt. True to his word, he very shortly stood up, shook my skirt out, and handed it back to me. He'd completely mended it with small, even stitches, and he'd done so in such a way that the original tear was imperceptible. I wasn't going to have to chuck the skirt after all.

It's been nearly eight years since my skirt was mended backstage at *Phantom*. I still have it, it's still in one piece, and the stitches are still holding fast.

Acting silly during a Phantom *performance.*

Le Sot

Many of the backstage crew members at *Phantom* were as generous and kind-hearted as the ones in Wardrobe department. Most of the staff and actors kept to themselves; the ones with whom we interacted were generally lovely.

The stage managers and others on the production team went out of their way to include the ushers, bartenders and merch sellers in all of the activities that went on around the theater. We were always invited to parties large and small; we always received production gifts at Christmas. One year it was a fleece red scarf embroidered with the *Phantom* logo. If you've seen the show you get this; if not, a red scarf plays a prominent role in Christine Daaé's back story. When I had friends visiting New York, the chief makeup artist was sometimes able to bring them backstage to meet the Phantom. One of the crew members even took some guests of mine on a backstage tour and let me climb to the top of the proscenium and walk around on the catwalk to see the golden angel up close.

During Girl Scout cookie season everyone stalked Felix. His daughter was a scout, and I have no doubt that she reached the top fundraising tier every year thanks to *Phantom*. Cast, crew and front of house alike bought boxes and boxes of cookies. Felix delivered full cases of Thin Mints and Tagalongs to some of us. Even after cookie time had wound down, you could occasionally find people wandering up to Felix's booth to ask if his daughter maybe, possibly, perhaps had any stray boxes that hadn't been sold. Felix and I both spoke French and liked the same baseball team; those two topics alone provided endless hours of deep conversation.

When Felix wasn't there, an Orthodox priest who happened to also be a theater tech sometimes covered his spot. One of the ushers would always ask him for a blessing. Since he was in a tiny booth for the entire show, Phil and I joked that he was the Priest in a Box. He took it in good humor.

There were only a handful of back of house folks who seemed openly contemptuous of the ushers. Unfortunately, one of these unpleasant individuals had the ability to directly impede the front of house staff, since he controlled access to the building as the day doorman. He flatly refused to allow ushers to enter the theater via the stage door. His stance was absolutely and totally wrong; the ushers had just as much of a right to use that entrance as any other employees, and company policy backed that up. This asshole, however, would actually make the ushers walk all the way around the block to the front of the Majestic instead of letting them go in through the stage door. He would also refuse to buzz them in when they rang the bell at the locked gate at the end of the stage door alley. For the rest of this essay, we shall refer to him as Le Sot, which essentially means "the fool" in French.

Fortunately, since he only worked days, I didn't have to interact with Le Sot very much. The night doorman was his polar opposite, as well. However, on matinee days Le Sot was a looming, hostile presence, and on one occasion he almost cost me a show's wages. I was on the C/E subway line en route to the matinee, and there was a major issue of some sort. My train stopped for several long minutes in the tunnel between stations, proceeded to trundle slowly right past my stop at 42nd Street, and didn't let anyone out until 50th Street. By the time I got out of the station it was nearly one, and I was a full five blocks from the Majestic. I had to be there by 1:05 if I wanted to work that day. With only five minutes to spare, I sprinted down 8th Avenue, dodging tourists and walking in the street to get ahead. I made it to the stage door gate with two minutes left.

I normally went into the theater through the front entrance on 44th Street, but there was no time left to run around the block, and I was far closer to the stage door on 45th. Unfortunately for me, Le Sot was on duty, and he refused to buzz me in. I knew he could see me on the security camera since I was standing right under it, but he completely ignored me, even though I frantically rang the bell several times. The alley was the gateway to three different venues' stage doors, and they all had the same camera feed, so eventually a doorman at one of the other theaters took pity on me and buzzed me through. I dashed into the Majestic with only a minute to spare.

"Can I help you?" Le Sot stood in the corridor with a sneer on his face. He was blocking my path to the front of the house. I'd been a regular staff member at *Phantom* for five years by that point, he'd seen me on numerous occasions when he had walked through the theater, and he knew damn well who I was. He was just going out of his way to be a complete and utter jackass. I didn't even try to be polite; I snapped, "Yeah, I work here," and made a break for the passdoor. The fact that Le Sot knew exactly who I was, and that I had a right to be there, was evidenced when he didn't send security after me. I reported to the chief at 1:05 exactly, and luckily, I was allowed to work.

I complained about the incident to the house manager later in the day, and I insisted that it needed to be pursued. Le Sot's pettiness, snobbery and prejudice against the front of house staff had nearly cost me a performance's pay.

I don't know if Le Sot is still at *Phantom*, and frankly, I don't care. I'm sure that wherever he is, the snarl on his face is still there and he's still looking down on others to make himself feel better.

Unfortunately, Le Sot wasn't the only nasty person at the Majestic. There were a few performers who made it clear that they couldn't stand us. Once when I was sitting in the inner lobby between shows I overheard two of the supporting actresses as they were walking by. They were talking about places to hold a gathering. One of them, who played Madam Giry, commented, "We could do it downstairs, but the *ushers* are there." Her tone of voice left no doubt as to her opinion of the ushers, and it wasn't positive. On another day I was nearly bowled over by a chorus actress who was, for some reason, running through the orchestra section to get backstage. There was no "Excuse me;" there was no "Hey, I'm sorry I just plowed right into you." I was just an usher; I didn't count.

Toward the end of my run at *Phantom* the negativity did override the happy moments. I detested the show, I disliked a fair number of my colleagues, and I hated being there. When I had to sit "inside" – i.e., remain inside the auditorium to watch for problems and guide patrons during the performance – I zoned out so I didn't have to focus on anything happening onstage. I waited outside the theater until 6:59 so I didn't spend even an extra minute there. I refused to work late on nights when they needed extra hands, even though there was double pay involved. I declined to be included in the group photos for *The Playbill Broadway Yearbook*. Simply put, I was done.

I referred to *Phantom* as "Omega" when I talked about it with friends. The code name was prophetic: as Omega was the last letter in the Greek alphabet, so would *Phantom* be my last Broadway show. And I was completely and totally fine with that.

Closing Night

Some people see the proverbial writing on the wall; I just saw myself in the mirror in vibrant color. About six years after I began ushering I started noticing changes in my patterns of dress. When I wasn't working I wore a lot of color. In fact, I didn't want to wear any black shirts or dresses on my days off at all. I was seeking out rainbow tie-dye and neon green. I wanted extreme brightness.

Two or three years into my time at *Phantom*, I also started withdrawing from ushering and the theatrical world. I no longer accepted invitations to see Broadway shows with friends, even when the tickets were free. I followed the lead of many of my colleagues and called out for two shows every single week.

Sometimes I had things to do. I was living more in the world and less in the theater; I was going to events all over the city. I went on a tour of the abandoned Atlantic Avenue Tunnel and explored the boarded-up parts of Governor's Island; I screamed at rock concerts and minor league Cyclones baseball games out in Brooklyn; I hung out with friends more often. I carried a banner and marched in the Coney Island Mermaid Parade; I held a huge puppet and marched up Sixth Avenue in the Village Halloween Parade. I even went back to working as an extra in films and played everything from a taxidermy customer to an Eastern European peasant.

My health, which had been extremely poor in the early 2000s, began to slowly improve. I didn't need a doctor to tell me; I could see it in the mirror. For about four years my face had been so bloated and distorted that I hadn't even recognized myself; now the real me seemed to be making a return appearance. Nobody had yet gotten to the heart of the chronic condition I had which flared up every so often, but being away from Broadway seemed to be the best medicine.

My personal Renaissance extended to my writing, which similarly had been in a holding pattern for several years. At seventeen I'd interviewed famous authors and politicians; at nineteen I'd been bold enough to write a book for UNICEF and had published articles in two countries; but by twenty-four, without any interference from anyone else, I'd completely lost my nerve and my confidence. I never stopped writing, but I stopped submitting it for publication. I wrote complete novels for National Novel Writing Month, known as NaNoWriMo online, saved them to my hard drive, and forgot about them.

As I emerged from my mental and physical chrysalis and pulled away from Broadway, my writing mojo returned. I started slowly, submitting pieces to newspapers and magazines here and there. In 2009 I placed an essay in *She's Shameless*, a Canadian book that would go on to be a featured selection in the Toronto Public Library's Word Out teen reading program. I followed that up with an acceptance to *Chicken Soup for the Soul: What I Learned from the Cat*. I was quoted in an edition of Lonely Planet's guidebook for the Languedoc-Roussillon region of France and contributed a painting to a fan book on The Cure. I was back.

I didn't tell my colleagues about my writing or any of my other activities outside of work, for the most part. The malicious sorts at *Phantom* were stuck on the idea that I was a loser with no life outside the theater, and far be it from me to deprive them of their delusions. They'd actually mocked me when they saw me come to the theater in a volunteer shirt one day. I'd spent the morning working at an event in support of the blind, and apparently that was somehow objectionable to them. I did bring copies of the *Shameless* and *Chicken Soup for the Soul* books to work and clandestinely showed them to a few supportive co-workers, though, and I was touched when they were proud and happy for me.

The more I lived, the more I understood that I didn't want the theater to be the focal point of my world anymore. I was tired of being treated horribly by patrons every day. I was weary of watching people emote onstage. I decided that I would much rather see things being accomplished in real life.

I was beginning to view things at *Phantom* far more clearly; to recognize and eschew the backbiting. The constant chatter on the grapevine, which had always been so entertaining, took on a sinister timbre. I limited my interactions with the more vicious gossips, and I became doubly vigilant about keeping my personal business to myself. The Broadway colleagues who had friended me on Facebook, for instance, were filtered out of almost all of my posts and photos about my activities outside of work.

An astrologer might have noted that I had approached Saturn Return, the period in one's late twenties when one's perspective and, often life, change. My mother would have simply said that I finally woke up, damn it. Whatever the reason for my sea change, the results were good. Even if I wasn't aware of it at first, my orbit was slowly but steadily shifting away from Broadway. Soon it would leave the theatrical galaxy altogether.

Puppeteering in the Village Halloween Parade.

The Pneumonia I Never Had

New Year's Day 2009 found me on the beach at Coney Island in a swimsuit, hopping around and rubbing my hands together to stay warm. Around me, hundreds of other swimmers were shivering in the Arctic January wind.

"Don't submerge your head. Try to keep your chest above water. Get in and then *get out*." A member of the Coney Island Polar Bear Club wandered through the crowd and shouted instructions. I took them to heart. The Polar Bears swam in the Atlantic every week even in the dead of winter. If *they* were saying it was too cold for more than a momentary dip, I was going to believe them.

As I shuffled back and forth in my flip-flops and prepared to run, I had a brief moment of lucidity. Why was I doing this, again? It raised money for a cancer charity, true. It was on my list of quirky New York things to do at least once, yes. However, I was about to plunge into the Atlantic Ocean in sub-zero temperatures in January. What the hell was wrong with me?

I knew, really. My cat, Chewie, was dying. That was not hyperbole. On New Year's Eve, the vet had told me that Chewie had between twenty-four hours and two weeks to live. He had successfully fought lymphoma, but now he was in the final stages of congestive heart failure and his lungs were full of fluid. They'd fixed him up with palliative care so I could take him home for another day to say goodbye to him, but he was about to make his exit. I didn't think it was going to be two weeks at all. It was

Thursday, and he was going to be lucky if he made it to Monday.

I'd had Chewie since I was in high school, and he was my best friend. If that sounds pathetic to you, you've never been lucky enough to own a "forever cat." Chewie had been with me through nearly every ordeal of my teenage and young adult life; he'd been patient and loving even when I had been hard to deal with, and he'd been a gift to me. Chewie had never let me down, and the idea of losing him was devastating. My interlude on the beach was actually one of the only times in the last day that I hadn't been crying.

I was running into the icy water because I didn't care about anything other than Chewie; because I was numb and I wanted to feel something again; because I cared so deeply that I was desperate for something to deaden the pain. It was all of the above and none of it. When the air horn sounded, I let out a battle cry and joined all the others who were charging toward the waves.

Pain. Oh yes, it hurt. I took care to follow the instructions I'd been given; I kept my head and chest well above the water. I bounced around for a few moments, hollered and cheered with the rest of the lunatics, and then scurried back toward the beach. A random man took a photo with me; it was a warm, fuzzy moment.

I had trouble putting my clothes back on because my hands were frozen into odd positions. I felt like the Elephant Man as I tried to maneuver my socks back onto my feet without the use of my fingers. Eventually I was bundled up again in warm, dry clothes. I trudged back to the subway, where the heated train cars were extremely welcome, and headed home. Chewie met me at the door.

It turned out to be his last stand. Before I went to work in the evening, where I showed everyone my insane Polar Bear photo, he was fine. His condition sharply declined in the middle of the night, and by the morning, when large doses of feline morphine were not making a dent for him, I knew he was on his way out.

By midday we were at the vet's office for Chewie's final journey. I stayed with him the entire time; there was no way I could have left. The vet let me sit with him as long as I wanted after he died. I finally returned to my apartment, put Chewie's toys and food dishes away, met my mother for lunch and completely lost it.

Why is this story in a book about Broadway? It was the pneumonia I never had.

Considering that I was going off on crying jags every few minutes and felt as though my heart had been smashed to pieces, there was no way I was going to be able to work at *Phantom*. Absolutely, positively none. It was a holiday weekend and we had extra performances, so my presence was sorely needed, but it was out of the question. I e-mailed Tom, the house manager at the Majestic, and Erin, my boss at the Shuberts. Both knew of Chewie's ongoing illness; both understood. They shared their own stories of losing beloved pets. The support I received from the Shuberts management after the death of my cat still ranks as one of the nicest, most compassionate things an employer has ever done for me.

New Year's Day, 2009: The Polar Bear Plunge that did not make me ill.

I asked both Erin and Tom to keep the situation confidential. They agreed. We all knew full well that some of the people working at Phantom were unbelievably petty and cruel, and that they would have used the situation as a springboard for their jokes and taunts.

When I finally did make it back to work several days later, I discovered that everyone thought that I'd gotten sick from my foray into the Atlantic. And numerous people had been happy about it. They'd chuckled and smiled and thought it was wonderful that I'd ended up with a dreadful respiratory illness. If that doesn't tell you how much these folks sucked, I don't know what will.

I never did tell any of them the real story. I privately grieved for Chewie, went about my business and smiled and nodded when my "lung infection" was mentioned. When I felt better I occasionally joked with the house manager about my bout of fictional pleurisy, sat back, and let the gossips dig themselves deeper into their pit of malice.

The Pneumonia I *Did* Have

In March 2010 I developed a respiratory infection for real. The X-rays showed bronchial cuffing; I was gasping for air and coughing up unpleasant substances. I was overjoyed, because I didn't have to go to *Phantom*. It had become that bad.

I'd long passed the point of letting other people's petty prejudices, judgments and venom poison me. I knew that some of my colleagues didn't like me. I'd wager that a few of them actually hated me, and I knew that those people spent a fair amount of time mocking me behind my back. I honestly didn't care. It was their wasted time, not mine. I found it pathetic and sad that they didn't have anything more interesting in their lives to fixate on.

All the same, dealing with it on a day-to-day basis was very draining. Here's an analogy. Let's say that you're locked in house where four-fifths of the people have the Black Plague. You happen to be among the twenty percent who aren't ill. The others who are healthy try to keep your spirits up, but being around so many who are riddled with Plague, and wondering what's going to hit you next, is understandably very emotionally exhausting. That's how it was at the tail end of my *Phantom* run. Even if I let the drama bounce off me, it was tiresome.

Getting a free pass to stay away from Broadway was a blessing to me, even though my time out was unpaid. I stayed home, took my antibiotics and tried to recuperate. To keep my strength up, and to compensate for the loss of the four-mile roundtrip walk I usually did to get to and from work, I bundled up every evening and took night walks. I tried to explore all the nooks and crannies of lower Manhattan, and ended up roaming through dim downtown streets with strange murals, old diners and quaint churches.

My efforts to return to *Phantom* were hellish because I wasn't fully recovered. Talking to patrons for a half hour used up precious air that I just didn't have. Walking up and down the aisles and staircases made me dizzy and used more air.

This was compounded by the fact that most of the time the head usher did little to nothing to help me. As a courtesy, ushers with illnesses or injuries were commonly placed in less hectic sections where they didn't have to walk as much. I, on the other hand, was automatically assigned to my regular spot in the front of the orchestra: the busiest place an usher could be. Adding insult to injury: business was slow, and some nights the other sections didn't have any patrons at all. I'd pause to cough, look toward the back of the house and see the ushers in those sections just standing around chatting since they didn't have any customers to seat. And meanwhile, since the front of the orchestra was always full, my aisle partner Penny and I were always scurrying around. Penny was one of the good guys at *Phantom* and she tried to help me as much as possible, but in the front of the orchestra we both needed to be quick and efficient. Sick or not, I wasn't going to let her shoulder that load on her own, so I did everything I could to keep up.

Every now and then it would dawn on the chief to ask me if I needed to be moved to a slower section, but the most part, I was tossed right back into the fire. And then my lungs broke down from the strain, I started coughing up junk again, and I ended up calling out for the rest of the week.

On the last Saturday I was scheduled to work at *Phantom*, I missed the matinee with an excruciating headache. The substitute house manager told me to take the night off to rest, too.

And that was that. I never went back. I never said goodbye.

On Monday I contacted Erin and told her I was done. I was asked to take a three-month leave to think about it, even though I really didn't want to return to the show. I didn't want to work at other theaters, either. I was done with ushering. I didn't care about the pay; I didn't care about the convenient schedule. I just didn't want to be there anymore. I told Erin point-blank that I didn't want a leave. I'm sure she was right to counsel caution, but I was also sure that I'd made up my mind. It didn't stick: two months later, the Shuberts wrote to me to ask if I was ready to return from my leave of absence. The chief actually called me. A few of the more hostile colleagues tracked me down on social media or emailed me to try to figure out where I'd gone.

I kept my word: I was done. I withdrew from the ushers' local of IATSE. I put my scarves and locker key in a manila envelope and dropped them off at the Majestic box office. I looked through my Facebook, picked out almost every friend or acquaintance that was a Broadway usher, sent them a goodbye note, and deleted them. None of the Broadway people had known anything that was actually happening in my life for quite some time since they were already on a tight filter. Still, given the way gossip went around the Theater District, and given that people on Broadway spent hours talking about the stupidest and most insignificant things, I didn't want any of them to be privy to *any* information about my life from that point on. As much as I liked some of them, I couldn't trust them to keep anything to themselves. My actions were justified a few days later when someone who hadn't even received the Facebook goodbye note asked me about it. The new gossip had already made the rounds. The only Broadway person I kept on Facebook, and in my life, was my spirit twin from *Cats* and *The Invention of Love*, Greg. He'd turned out to be a true friend.

I never did get to say farewell to the orchestra team at *Phantom* or the other people I liked there, like Felix. That was a shame, but it was what it was.

When I healed up and started surfing through job ads online, I quickly came across a listing for Cirque du Soleil's *Ovo*. They weren't seeking performers; they were looking for people to work in their front of house, selling merchandise. It was essentially retail work in a cool setting. I scored an interview and was hired on the spot.

Ovo was a tough gig. The work was more physical than ushering had been, Cirque du Soleil's rules were stricter, and I had far more to do. My commute to *Phantom* had been about thirty minutes on foot; to get to Cirque du Soleil I needed to leave an hour and a half to be safe. The circus was set up on Randall's Island, which was quite a distance from my apartment on the West Side. Every day I walked across town to the train on Lexington Avenue, disembarked at 125th Street, and trekked over the Triboro Bridge on foot to get to work. At night such journeys were not necessarily safe, so I needed two buses and a train to get home. I waited for the M23 at midnight, under the reassuring glow of the sign from the 24-hour Walgreens on Lexington and 23rd.

On the last day of the New York run, the Powers That Be fitted us with hard hats and vests and asked if we would help them take the tents down, so I actually had the experience of disassembling a circus. And I had a blast.

At the end of *The Phantom of the Opera*, the Phantom vanishes. He simply sits down on his throne and goes away. I left Broadway the same way, really: one day I was there; one day I wasn't.

Working at Cirque du Soleil.

Epilogue

There's a persistent belief that native or long-time New Yorkers can't leave their city. I dispute that. Even though I mostly grew up in the heart of New York City and graduated from both high school and college there, I took my leave from the East Coast in late 2010. I haven't regretted it. I'm glad I left. I think I'm in the Henry Miller camp, a.k.a. the New Yorkers who leave, have absolutely no wish to return even to visit, and never live there again.

When I'm asked if there's anything I really miss about New York, my list is short: a) my family; b) my friends; c) the pizza; d) the Brooklyn Cyclones; and e) the Metropolitan Museum of Art. The city I knew and loved in the 80s, 90s and early 2000s just doesn't exist anymore, and I don't like the gentrified, unaffordable, cookie-cutter version that has sprung up in its place. Most of my favorite haunts – the old greasy spoon diners, L'Amour, CBGB, Love Saves the Day and the Barnes & Noble bookstore on Avenue of the Americas, among others – are long gone.

I've fully adapted to my new chosen city and state, I love the way of life here, and I can't imagine leaving. I avoid visiting New York as much as possible. In 2014, however, I flew back to support a relative during a major medical crisis. Along the way, I managed to reconcile with some old friends and perhaps, as the talk shows would say, gained some closure.

In midtown I walked past the Belasco Theatre, which had been grandly restored in my absence. A quick peek into the box office lobby revealed that even the sagging, warped bottle-glass near the front door had been repaired. Thankfully, even after the extensive renovations, David Belasco's portrait maintained its place of honor on the wall. Outside there was a line of fans waiting for standby tickets to that night's performances of *Hedwig and the Angry Inch*. I took a selfie in front of the marquee and said a silent hello to David. I could just imagine how thrilled he was to see that his theater had been returned to its original splendor, with a 2010s twist.

However, aside from my visit to the Belasco and a quick stroll past the Winter Garden, I made a point of staying out of the Theater District. I didn't want to run into anyone I'd once known, regardless if I liked them. I'd done a very clean job of extricating myself from that world.

Still, my old friend Greg and I had coffee together on the time-honored theatrical schedule: between matinee and evening performances on a Wednesday. We arranged to meet in a location that was near enough to the Theater District to be accessible for Greg and far enough away to be comfortable for me: Bryant Park. It was a joyful reunion. Greg and I share that special talent that is perhaps exclusive to very good friends: the ability to sit down and immediately start talking comfortably, as if we've last seen each other four days ago instead of four years. At the mention of *The Invention of Love*, we simultaneously burst out: "Worst show EVER!"

One of the only things I regretted about my time in the theater, or rather, my exit from it, was that I never said goodbye to the handful of ushers at *Phantom* who had been both kind and fair to me. I just vanished. I had to right that wrong, so I asked Greg to give them a note from me, with my hugs and best wishes.

At the afternoon turned into the evening, Greg needed to head back to work, so we bid farewell to each other. A week later I said goodbye to New York as I boarded a plane. When I landed on the West Coast again, as clichéd as it sounds, I actually did want to kiss the ground.

Still. . . Broadway seems to creep up on me sometimes.

It popped up during my job at a museum, where one of my duties was to facilitate tours with young people. The topics were heavy; we discussed genocide, human rights and the civil rights movement in the United States, among other subjects.

During one tour I had a group of Drama Club students who were staging a production of *Cabaret*. It was an edgy choice for high school, and I was impressed that the teachers and administration were going for it.

The kids clustered in front of a photo of Anne Frank at her desk. We were talking about artistic outlets, and about the fact that Anne's famous diary had been one. Some people dive into art, sports, video games, TV or theater; Anne had found her oasis in writing.

"What does the Emcee say in your show?" I asked the kids. "What's one of his first lines?" I didn't wait for them to answer. "*'We have no troubles here. Here, life is beautiful.'*" The teenagers murmured; I'd plucked the phrase verbatim out of thin air, complete with a faux-German accent. After all, there's no way to quote the Emcee without it. Museum docents didn't generally break out the Broadway on them.

When the Emcee invites you into the cabaret, he never says that things will go smoothly. The dancers have track marks and sunken eyes; their smiles look malevolent in the dim lighting. If you stay there too long you'll become one of them, too. The Emcee doesn't guarantee that you will leave the nightclub unscathed. He only promises you that you will forget about the outside world, and perhaps leave with a greater understanding of what you see through the lens of your life. He's right.

The theater. Ushering. There, life was beautiful. Flawed, viciously, beautiful. I'm eternally grateful that I had a front row seat at that cabaret for such a very long time. I'm even more grateful that I got away from it.

Front of House

Bibliography

Belasco, David. *Return of Peter Grimm, The* (Novelization). New York: Grosset and Dunlap, 1912.

Belasco, David. *Six Plays*. Boston: Little, Brown and Co., 1928.

Belasco, David. *Theatre Through Its Stage Door, The*. New York and London: Harper & Brothers Publishing, 1919.

Botto, Louis and Viagas, Robert. *At This Theatre*. New York: Applause Books, 2002.

Eaton Travis, Doris and Morris, J.M. *The Days We Danced*. Seattle: Marquant Press, 2003.

Frayn, Michael. *Copenhagen*. 1998.

"Lyceum Theatre." Shubert Organization, www.shubert.nyc/theatres/lyceum.

Masteroff, Joe. *Cabaret*. Lyrics and music by John Kander and Fred Ebb. 1966.

Morrison, William. *Broadway Theaters: History and Architecture*. New York: Dover Publications, 1999.

Pickford, Mary. *Sunshine and Shadow*. New York: Doubleday and Co., 1955.

van Hoogstraten, Nicholas. *Lost Broadway Theatres*. New York: Princeton Architectural Press, 1997.

Webber, Andrew Lloyd and Stilgoe, Richard. *Phantom of the Opera, The*. Lyrics and music by Andrew Lloyd Webber, Charles Hart and Richard Stilgoe. 1986.

About the Author

Denise Reich is an Italian-born, New York City-raised American-European freelance writer and photographer. She currently contributes to the Canadian magazine *Shameless*. Her work has appeared in publications in the USA, Canada, Bermuda, South Africa and Eastern Europe, and has been translated into several languages.

During her years as a Broadway usher Denise worked at more than fifty different productions in twenty-five theaters, including *Cats*, *The Phantom of the Opera*, *Def Poetry Jam*, *Art*, *Enchanted April* and many others. During the same period of time she completed her four-year degree, did post-graduate work, traveled to five continents, was published in numerous magazines and books, went through four operations, and lived in seven different places.

Denise currently lives on the West Coast and drinks lots of Café du Monde coffee. She holds a BA from Marymount Manhattan College and has also studied in California, France and South Africa.

Denise can be found on Twitter at @WriterDenise or on her website, **www.freewebs.com/denisenox**.

www.ingramcontent.com/pod-product-compliance
Lightning Source LLC
Chambersburg PA
CBHW031347040426
42444CB00005B/221